Becoming Money $mart

by

Judi Deatherage

Publisher
The Goodheart-Willcox Company, Inc.
Tinley Park, Illinois
www.g-w.com

Copyright © 2012
by
The Goodheart-Willcox Company, Inc.

All rights reserved. No part of this work may be reproduced, stored, or transmitted in any form or by any electronic or mechanical means, including information storage and retrieval systems, without the prior written permission of
The Goodheart-Willcox Company, Inc.

Manufactured in the United States of America.

ISBN 978-1-60525-470-8

3 4 5 6 7 8 9 – 12 – 16 15 14 13

The Goodheart-Willcox Company, Inc. Brand Disclaimer: Brand names, company names, and illustrations for products and services included in this text are provided for educational purposes only and do not represent or imply endorsement or recommendation by the author or the publisher.

The Goodheart-Willcox Company, Inc. Safety Notice: The reader is expressly advised to carefully read, understand, and apply all safety precautions and warnings described in this book or that might also be indicated in undertaking the activities and exercises described herein to minimize risk of personal injury or injury to others. Common sense and good judgment should also be exercised and applied to help avoid all potential hazards. The reader should always refer to the appropriate manufacturer's technical information, directions, and recommendations; then proceed with care to follow specific equipment operating instructions. The reader should understand these notices and cautions are not exhaustive.

The publisher makes no warranty or representation whatsoever, either expressed or implied, including, but not limited to, equipment, procedures, and applications described or referred to herein, their quality, performance, merchantability, or fitness for a particular purpose. The publisher assumes no responsibility for any changes, errors, or omissions in this book. The publisher specifically disclaims any liability whatsoever, including any direct, indirect, incidental, consequential, special, or exemplary damages resulting, in whole or in part, from the reader's use or reliance upon the information, instructions, procedures, warnings, cautions, applications or other matter contained in this book. The publisher assumes no responsibility for the activities of the reader.

Introduction

Financial Capability—What Does It Mean to You?

As a young adult, one of the most important keys to your success will be financial capability. Being financially capable means you understand topics related to finance such as making money, spending money, and saving money wisely. With our rapidly changing economy, it has become clear that as a young person, you will need to learn how to make wise financial decisions at an early age. Wise financial decisions will help you lead a productive life, as well as enable you to be a positive contributor to the economic stability of the nation.

As you progress through *Becoming Money $mart*, you will have many opportunities to learn about financial capability—how it impacts your life now and how it will influence your future. As you read each new topic, you will have a chance to jump in and see how the information applies to you as a student. You will learn how to make your money work for you and how to plan for your career and your future.

So have fun as you begin the journey and learn how to become money smart!

About the Author

Judi Deatherage is a retired business education teacher from Kentucky with a passion for educating teens about money. She received her Master's Degree from the University of Cincinnati and her Bachelor's Degree from Eastern Kentucky University. During her teaching career, Judi taught accounting and finance courses to high school and college students. She was the recipient of Ashland Oil's Golden Apple Award for Teachers and is listed in Who's Who Among America's Teachers. Judi is the author of a trade book, *Who Wants to be a Millionaire*, which focuses on basic principles of financial literacy for teens.

To the Student

There is much to learn about becoming money smart. Financial capability starts here.

Terms

Terms are highlighted in the chapter to help build your business vocabulary.

Your Financial IQ

Your Financial IQ opens each chapter to evaluate what you already know about the financial topic to be presented.

Objectives

Objectives are correlated to the main chapter headings to define your goals for learning the content.

Web Connect

Web Connect leads you to the Internet to develop your research skills.

Dollars and $ense

Dollars and $ense highlights tips for being financially savvy and how to relate these topics to your everyday life.

FYIs provide financial facts to enhance what you have learned.

To the Student

As you progress through the material, it is important to assess what you have learned. Self-assessment will help you identify financial concepts that need more attention so that you will have a clearer understanding of each.

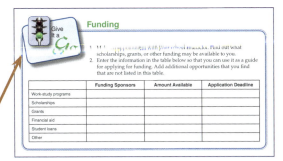

Give It a Go

Give It a Go gives you an opportunity for a hands-on activity to apply what you have learned.

Check Your Understanding

Check Your Understanding provides self-assessment activities to make sure you understand the topic before progressing to the next section.

You Do the Math

You Do the Math problems demonstrate financial concepts with an opportunity for you to apply the math you have learned.

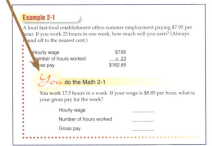

Being Financially Responsible

Being Financially Responsible asks if you are prepared to create a financial plan and look ahead to your future.

Chapter Summaries

Chapter summaries provide an overview so that you may gain a reinforcement of chapter content.

End-of-Chapter Activities

End-of-chapter activities, including a Math Skill Builder, enable you to review what you have learned in the chapter.

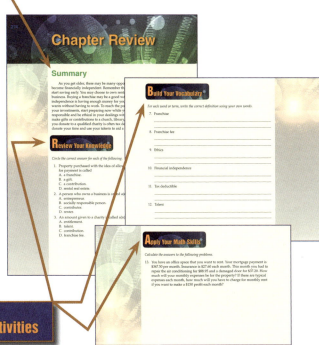

Table of Contents

Chapter 1   Planning Your Financial Future:
It Begins Here..................................7

Chapter 2   Paychecks: Using Your Money Wisely............30

Chapter 3   Budgeting: Keeping Track of Your Money........60

Chapter 4   Banking: Managing Your Money.................81

Chapter 5   Credit: Buy Now, Pay Later...................114

Chapter 6   Insurance: Protecting Your Assets............138

Chapter 7   Education: A Passport to Your Future.........164

Chapter 8   Loans: Cars and Housing......................185

Chapter 9   Investments: Making Your Money
Work for You................................208

Chapter 10   Retirement Planning: Looking
Toward the Future...........................238

Chapter 11   Your Financial Future: You Make the Choice....261

Glossary..277

Index...285

1 Planning Your Financial Future: It Begins Here

Terms

Financial plan
Financial goals
Needs
Wants
Values
Wealth
Net worth
Assets
Liabilities
Investing
Financial independence
Growth
Average rate of return
Interest

Compound interest
Principal
Simple interest
Rule of 72

Objectives

When you complete Chapter 1, you will be able to:

- **Explain** the purpose of a financial plan.
- **Define** *wealth* and calculate net worth.
- **Define** *investing* and calculate average rate of return and compound interest.

Your Financial IQ

Before you read this chapter, answer the following questions to see how much you already know about financial planning and investing.

1. What does it mean to save money? What does it mean to invest money? How are these two things similar, yet different?

2. What does it mean to be financially independent?

3. What does financial planning mean?

4. Are you saving money now? If so, how long have you had a savings account? What rate of interest are you earning? How often is the interest being compounded?

5. Do you keep track of how much you spend each week and how much you save? How would this impact your financial goals?

6. What does financial literacy mean to you? Why will this be important in your goals and plans for the future?

7. What is the best way to build wealth? When should you start?

8. How important is having your own spending money?

9. By tracking how you spend your money, do you think you could spend your money more wisely?

10. What items could you do without now in order to begin saving more money for your future?

Financial Planning

You, as a teen or young adult, have been using money for much of your life. Do you think about where your money goes or how you're spending it? Do you think about saving money? You have a responsibility to use your money wisely. Teens and young adults can be responsible with their money if given the right information. You are accountable for your future.

Have you heard of the term financial planning? A **financial plan** is a set of goals for acquiring, saving, and spending money. The plan also includes actions or strategies for achieving the goals. Do you want to just "get by" and live from paycheck to paycheck throughout your life, or do you want to be free from financial worry? Will you leave your financial security to chance or follow a plan for acquiring and spending money? Having a financial plan helps you be in control of your financial situation and achieve your goals.

This text will give you information you need to begin a lifetime financial plan and start you on your way to becoming financially secure. Some of the information may be familiar to you; some may be completely new. In either case, the information will be valuable in securing your financial future. You are now on your way to becoming money smart.

Why is financial planning important?

_____
_____
_____
_____

Financial Goals

Goals are something that you work toward or strive to achieve. **Financial goals** are measurable objectives related to acquiring or spending money. You may have simple short-term goals, such as buying a new shirt or a gift for your friend's birthday. Other short-term goals might be to earn money and purchase a car. Long-term goals might include buying a house or retiring at age 50.

Setting goals is an important first step in creating a financial plan. Planning is essential before financial goals can be met. Most people do not have enough money to buy everything they want without planning and saving their money. For example, a family paying for a child's college education probably did not start saving money when the child was 16 or 17. They probably began saving years earlier and have made sacrifices to save enough to achieve this goal.

You will always have choices to make with your money. You may have to give up things you want now in order to be financially secure later. Setting both short-term and long-term goals now will help you achieve many things you want for your future.

Check Your Understanding

How are financial goals different from other goals you may have?

_____
_____
_____
_____

Dollars and $ense

SMART Goals

Financial planning is an important process that will guide you in the future. You should begin by creating a financial plan now. The plan will help you make wise decisions for saving and spending money as you move through your working years. Have you ever heard of SMART goals? SMART is an acronym for:

❑ Specific
❑ Measurable
❑ Attainable
❑ Relevant
❑ Timely

Many organizations use SMART goals to help employees focus on performing work tasks. Use this SMART chart as you set reasonable short- and long-term goals for your financial plan.

S	• Are my short- and long-term goals **specific**? • Exactly what do I want to achieve?
M	• Are my goals **measureable**? • How will I know when a goal is achieved?
A	• Are my goals **attainable**? • Am I setting goals that can be achieved?
R	• Are my goals **relevant** to meeting my financial needs? • Will meeting the goals help me become financially secure?
T	• Are my goals **timely**? • Are the dates for achieving my goals appropriate?

Needs and Wants

Before you can set financial goals, you must determine your needs and wants. **Needs** are those things a person must have to survive, such as food, water, shelter, and clothing. One of your financial goals may be to have enough money to pay for your basic needs. In addition to needs, most people have lots of wants. **Wants** are things a person desires but are not necessary for survival. Examples of wants include cell phones, cars, designer clothes, etc. (Although some people may argue that cell phones are needs, you can see the difference!) A financial goal that many people have is to purchase a car.

In many cases, wants are related to values. **Values** are your beliefs about ideas and principles that are important to you. For example, a value for you might be honesty. A value for someone else might be trustworthiness. Have you thought about your values? Values are different for everyone. Your experiences and the ideas and beliefs of your family and friends may affect your values. Your values will affect how you think about money. If you value helping others, for example, you may be likely to give money to charities or to friends who are in need.

By considering your values and then prioritizing your needs and wants, you can direct your financial future. If you are like most people, you will desire things that are not needs. If you spend too much money on things you want, you might not have enough money to pay for things you need. By understanding the difference between needs and wants, you can make informed, reasonable choices based on the money you have available.

F.Y.I.
Many people around the world struggle to obtain basic daily needs that others take for granted.

Check Your Understanding

Why is it important to know the difference between needs and wants? How do values play a role in determining needs and wants?

_____
_____
_____
_____
_____
_____
_____

Values, Wants, and Needs

Before you create a financial plan, you should consider your values.

1. On the table that follows, list 10 values that are very important to you. State how each value will influence you in earning, saving, or spending money.

Values	Influence

2. As part of a financial plan, you need to set your short-term and long-term goals. List 10 short-term goals that you would like to achieve. (Remember to consider your values when setting goals.) State actions you will take to achieve the goals and include the amount of money you may need.

Short-Term Goals	Actions and Money Needed

3. List 10 long-term goals that you would like to achieve. (Remember to consider your values when setting goals.) State actions you will take to achieve the goals and include the amount of money you may need.

Long-Term Goals	Actions and Money Needed

Building Wealth

Wealth, as it relates to finances, is a plentiful supply of money or valuable goods. A wealthy person may be called prosperous or affluent. Someone who is wealthy has enough money to be secure financially. Even someone who is wealthy may not necessarily have enough money to buy everything she or he desires. (Very few people can buy everything they want.) However, when you are wealthy, you do not have to worry about paying your bills.

As you begin a financial plan, you need to know your net worth. **Net worth** is the difference between what you own and what you owe. Net worth is found by listing all **assets** (things you own) and then subtracting **liabilities** (debts you owe) from the assets.

Assets – Liabilities = Net Worth

Where do you want to be financially in twenty or thirty years? Do you want to be on your way to becoming a millionaire or maybe already there? What makes someone a millionaire? Is it having $1 million or more in the bank? Not necessarily. An individual may have money in a bank and other assets that total $1 million or more. However, to be a millionaire, you must have a net worth of $1 million or more, not just $1 million in assets. Many people who earn large salaries or make money from investments never become millionaires because they have a large amount of debt. To give you a simple example, if you own a house worth $1 million, does that make you a millionaire? Not if you have a $900,000 mortgage on it! Get the idea?

F.Y.I.
Ideally, the older you are, the more your net worth should be. Your assets should increase while your liabilities decrease.

Building wealth is not as difficult as you may think; however, it does not happen overnight. Building wealth is usually not a matter of luck. It requires careful planning and wise decision making. Building wealth is possible even with a moderate income. Right now you may not be thinking beyond college or getting your first job. However, teens and young adults have a great advantage in their ability to build wealth. That advantage is youth. Time is on your side.

Example 1-1

If your total assets are $1,785 and your total liabilities are $968, what is your net worth?

Assets	$1,785.00
Liabilities	− 968.00
Net worth	$817.00

You Do the Math 1-1

If your total assets are $3,940 and your total liabilities are $1,232, what is your net worth?

Assets	_____
Liabilities	_____
Net worth	_____

Check Your Understanding

How is it possible to have a large amount of assets but only a modest net worth?

_____
_____
_____

Net Worth

You probably have some assets. Perhaps you have a cell phone, cash, money in a savings account, jewelry, sports equipment, video games, or other things of value. As part of your financial plan, you need to prepare a net worth statement.

1. List the assets you own and the amount each one is worth. Be aware that many items you own are probably no longer worth their purchase price. List an amount you could probably get for an item if you sold it. List the amounts of money you have in cash or in bank accounts.

Assets	Amounts
	$
	$
	$
	$
	$
	$
	$
	$
Total Value of Assets	$

2. List any liabilities you have and the amount for each one.

Liabilities	Amounts
	$
	$
	$
	$
Total Amount of Liabilities	$

3. Subtract your total liabilities from your total assets to find your net worth.

Assets	$
Liabilities	$
Net Worth	$

Investing

When creating a financial plan, many people decide to invest some of their money. **Investing** is putting money to a use that you hope will increase its value over time. Placing money in a savings account, buying savings bonds, or buying part ownership in a company are examples of investing. You can begin to invest at an early age and start to build wealth for your financial security in later years. If your investments are very successful, you may achieve financial independence. **Financial independence** is having enough money for your basic needs and modest wants without having to work.

Building wealth does not happen overnight, but requires long-range planning.

Shutterstock

Growth

Most people invest hoping for **growth**, or increase in value, of their investments over a period of years. Investing for growth is not a "get rich quick" scheme, but it is a simple plan for building wealth. Because most investments are not guaranteed, there is risk involved. Money placed in a savings account is insured for up to $250,000 per account by the Federal Deposit Insurance Agency (FDIC). The FDIC is an independent agency of the United States government. This type of investment is considered very safe. However, when interest rates are low, the investment will have low growth. Other types of investments, such as buying stocks in a company, may provide higher growth. These investments can be risky since there is no guaranteed rate of return as with a savings account.

Although it is never too late to start planning for financial independence, teen years are an ideal time to begin investing. Figure 1-1 shows two amazing examples of why it is important to begin investing at an early age.

In example A, suppose you invest $2,000 a year for 10 years starting at age 19. Then you stop investing money. The money grows at a rate of 10% per year. At age 65, you will have $1,083,959. That's more than $1 million from your investment of only $20,000. WOW!

In example B, suppose you begin at age 28 and invest $2,000 per year until you are age 65—a total of 38 years. At the same rate of 10%, you will have $728,087 from an investment of $76,000. This is still not bad, but check the math. You have invested $56,000 more and end up with $355,872 less.

To benefit from your investments later in life, start investing when you are young. Keep investing as much as you can even when doing so is difficult. You'll be glad you did!

Check *Your* Understanding

What does the word *growth* mean as it relates to investing?

___

___

Figure 1-1 Investment examples.

Example A		Example B	
Annual investment for 10 years	$2,000	Annual investment for 38 years	$2,000
Investment period	48 Years	Investment period	38 Years
Annual earnings rate	10%	Annual earnings rate	10%
Total investment	$20,000	Total investment	$76,000
Final amount	$1,083,959	Final amount	$728,087

Average Rate of Return

Savings and other investments normally do not earn the same rate of return each year over a long period of time. The rate varies over the years. One year you may earn 2%; the next year you may earn 5%. The **average rate of return** is the percentage that your savings or other investments earn over a period of time. To find the average rate of return, add the amount of increase or decrease for each year and get a total. Then divide the total by the number of years of the investment to get the average return amount. Divide the average return amount by the number of years to get the average rate of return.

Total Amount Earned ÷ Number of Years = Average Return Amount

Average Return Amount ÷ Number of Years = Average Rate of Return

There is no guaranteed rate of return on most types of investments. The return on stocks and interest rates go up and down. When investing over a period of 30 to 35 years, an average rate of return of 7% to 9% is not unrealistic. Suppose you are considering an investment in company stock. You should look at the rate of return for the past several years if possible. Doing so will give you a better idea of how your investment is likely to grow than just looking at the rate of return for the previous year or two.

Example 1-2

Negative numbers are shown in parentheses and represent losses for those years.

Investment $1,500

Year	Amount
1	$75.00
2	50.00
3	100.00
4	100.00
5	75.00
6	50.00
7	(50.00)
8	(25.00)
9	25.00
10	50.00
11	100.00
12	150.00
13	135.00
14	140.00
15	+ 125.00
Total amount	$1,100.00
Number of years	÷ 15
Average return amount	$73.33
Number of years	÷ 15
Average rate of return	4.89%

You Do the Math 1-2

Investment $1,000

Year	Amount
1	$100.00
2	75.00
3	85.00
4	100.00
5	75.00
6	75.00
7	70.00
8	(25.00)
9	(50.00)
10	+ 40.00

Total amount _____

Number of years _____

Average return amount _____

Number of years _____

Average rate of return _____

Check Your Understanding

Why is average rate of return an important concept for you to understand?

_____
_____
_____

Compound Interest

You probably already understand the concept of interest. **Interest** is a fee paid on borrowed money or money earned on deposits with a bank or other financial institution. The longer you keep money on deposit, the more you will earn.

To understand how time can make such a difference in your earnings, you need to understand compound interest. **Compound interest** is earning interest on the **principal** (amount invested) plus the interest you have already earned. For example, suppose you deposit $1,000 at an interest rate of 5%. In one year you will have $1,050. The next year, you will earn interest on $1,050 instead of $1,000. The interest will be $52.50 instead of $50.

Principal × Rate × Time = Interest

F.Y.I.
Interest rates are always stated as one-year percentages. To calculate interest, you must first convert the percentage to a decimal. For example, an interest rate of 5% would be converted to .05. A rate of 3.25% would be .0325

Results are amazing when you keep adding to your original investment amount on a regular basis. The younger you are when you start, the more your money grows during your working years. Money earned from compounding of interest over a period of 30 years really adds up. That's why it's called the magic of compounding!

To get an estimate of how much a one-time deposit of $1,000 can grow for you, use the following table and write your age in the blanks. This, of course, does not take into account any additions to your principal. Think what you could do with just $1,000 added each year!

Year	Age	5% Interest	11% Interest
Current Age		$1,000	$1,000
Current Age + 10 yrs.		$1,629	$2,839
Current Age + 20 yrs.		$2,653	$8,062
Current Age + 30 yrs.		$4,322	$22,892
Current Age + 40 yrs.		$7,040	$65,001
Current Age + 50 yrs.		$11,467	$184,565

The idea is to let your money grow without using it for a period of 20 to 30 years. You do need accounts that allow you to use your money for emergencies. However, you also need long-term savings that build for your financial independence and retirement. If you choose to keep working after you reach retirement age, that's fine. You may also choose to work part-time in your retirement years. Ideally though, continuing to work should be a choice and not a necessity.

Example 1-3

An example of compound interest is shown in the table below. For each year, the beginning balance is multiplied by the interest rate of 5%. That amount is added to the beginning balance. The ending balance then becomes the beginning balance for the next year.

Year	Beginning Balance	5% Interest	Ending Balance
1	$1,000.00	$50.00	$1,050.00
2	1,050.00	52.50	1,102.50
3	1,102.50	55.13	1,157.63
4	1,157.63	57.88	1,215.51
5	1,215.51	60.78	1,276.29

How much interest was earned?

Ending balance $1,276.29
Beginning balance − 1,000.00
Interest earned $276.29

Without compounding, interest would be $50 per year, for a total of $250. Interest that does not compound is called **simple interest**.

You Do the Math 1-3

Assume you deposit $5,000 in a saving account at an interest rate of 6% compounded annually. Calculate your earnings using the following table.

Year	Beginning Balance	6% Interest	Ending Balance
1	$5,000.00		
2			
3			
4			
5			

How much interest have you earned in the five-year period?

Ending balance   _____

Beginning balance   _____

Interest earned   _____

The results may not seem impressive in the first few years; but after 25 or 30 years, the difference is astounding. If you keep adding to your investment on a regular basis, the results are even better!

Check Your Understanding

How does compound interest differ from simple interest?

_____

_____

_____

Example 1-4

Now look at adding more to your investment along with compounding quarterly instead of annually. Suppose your initial deposit of $2,000 is compounded quarterly (four times per year) at 4% and you are depositing an additional $500 each quarter.

Step 1   Principal × Rate × Time = Interest

     $2,000 × .04 × .25 (1/4 of a year) = $20

Step 2   Principal + Interest = New Balance

     $2,000 + $20 = $2,020

Step 3   New balance + Deposit = 1st Quarter Balance

     $2,020 + $500 = $2,520

(This number is also the beginning balance for next quarter.)

Look at the following example to see how quickly your money can grow over a period of three years.

Year	Quarter	Principal	4% Rate	Time .25	New Balance	Deposit	Quarter Balance
1	1	$2,000.00	$80.00	$20.00	$2,020.00	$500.00	$2,520.00
1	2	2,520.00	100.80	25.20	2,545.20	500.00	3,045.20
1	3	3,045.20	121.81	30.45	3,075.65	500.00	3,575.65
1	4	3,575.65	143.03	35.76	3,611.41	500.00	4,111.41
2	1	4,111.41	164.46	41.11	4,152.52	500.00	4,652.52
2	2	4,652.52	186.10	46.53	4,699.05	500.00	5,199.05
2	3	5,199.05	207.96	51.99	5,251.04	500.00	5,751.04
2	4	5,751.04	230.04	57.51	5,808.55	500.00	6,308.55
3	1	6,308.55	252.34	63.09	6,371.63	500.00	6,871.63
3	2	6,871.63	274.87	68.72	6,940.35	500.00	7,440.35
3	3	7,440.35	297.61	74.40	7,514.75	500.00	8,014.75
3	4	8,014.75	320.59	80.15	8,094.90	500.00	8,594.90

Amazing, isn't it? For most savings accounts, the interest is compounded daily, which makes your money grow even faster.

You Do the Math 1-4

Now, you try it. Begin with a deposit of $3,500 and deposit an additional $300 each quarter. Your interest rate is 5% compounded quarterly for a period of three years.

Year	Quarter	Principal	4% Rate	Time .25	New Balance	Deposit	Quarter Balance
1	1	$3,500.00					
1	2						
1	3						
1	4						
2	1						
2	2						
2	3						
2	4						
3	1						
3	2						
3	3						
3	4						

Check Your Understanding

How does adding to your investment each year (or more often) affect the results of your investment?

_____
_____
_____

Current Interest Rates

1. Go to the Internet and find the websites for five savings institutions. What rates are they currently paying on savings accounts? Typically, the interest rate and an APY (annual percentage yield) are shown. Record both rates along with any minimum balance required and related fees.

Savings Institution	Interest Rate	APY	Minimum Balance	Fees

2. What is the purpose of showing an APY? Search the Internet to learn how using this number can help you when comparing investments.

_____
_____
_____
_____
_____

Rule of 72

Have you ever heard the term Rule of 72? The **Rule of 72** is an equation that lets you estimate how long it will take to double your investment with a fixed annual interest rate. To use the Rule of 72, divide 72 by the annual rate of return to find the number of years it will take to double your investment. Note that the Rule of 72 gives an estimate—not the exact answer. However, it is useful for quick mental calculations. Naturally, the higher the interest rate, the fewer number of years it will take to double your money.

72 ÷ Interest Rate = Number of Years to Double an Investment

Suppose that you are saving for college, and you have $5,000. You wonder if you could double this by the time you start college in three years. You found a great deal at a local bank for 4.5% interest on a savings account.

72 ÷ 4.5 = 16 years
(Do not convert the interest rate to a decimal for this calculation.)

The equation shows that you cannot double your money at this interest rate in three years. This is another reminder that planning for future needs or wants is important.

> **F.Y.I.**
> For you math wizards, the formula for compounding is $A = P(1 + r \div n)^{nt}$ where **P** is the original principal, **r** is the annual rate of interest, **t** is the number of years (time), and **n** is the number of times it is compounded in a year. **A**, of course, is the final amount. Remember, this assumes that you are putting all your money into your investment at one time, and not adding to it later.

Example 1-5

Your rate of return is 6%. How many years will it take for you to double your investment?

Start with	72
Divide by the interest rate	÷ 6
Number of years to double	12 years

You Do the Math 1-5

If the interest rate is 3%, how many years will it take for you to double your investment?

Start with	_____
Divide by the interest rate	_____
Number of years to double	_____

Check Your Understanding

Why would you use the Rule of 72 if the answer will not be exact?

_____
_____

Chapter 1   Planning Your Financial Future: It Begins Here

Financial Calculators

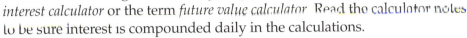

1. Go to the Internet and do a search for a financial calculator. There are many good financial calculators that are available online. Look for one that calculates compound interest daily over a period of years. You may need to search using the term *daily compound interest calculator* or the term *future value calculator*. Read the calculator notes to be sure interest is compounded daily in the calculations.
2. Using the table that follows and the online financial calculator, calculate the ending balances using the interest rates and the number of years given.

Deposit	Annual Interest Rate	Number of Years	Compounded	Ending Balance
$1,000	5%	20	Daily	
$2,000	3%	15	Daily	
$3,000	2%	25	Daily	

Needs and Wants
A Checklist

Do you ever think about what you really need and what you want? Use this checklist to help you consider your needs and wants.

Yes   No

1. Do I need to buy new clothes to look presentable?
2. Do I need to buy a car to get to school?
3. Do I need to save money for college?
4. Do I need to buy the latest DVDs?
5. Do I need to go the movies?
6. Do I have to borrow money to make it through the week?
7. Do I need to buy the newest video games?
8. Do I need to buy special sports equipment for the teams I play on?
9. Do I need a salon haircut?
10. Do I need to go out to eat with my friends every Friday night?

Chapter Review

Summary

A financial plan is a set of goals for acquiring, saving, and spending money. The plan also includes actions or strategies for achieving the goals. Following a financial plan can help you build wealth for financial security with even a modest income. When creating a financial plan, many people decide to invest some of their money. If your investments are very successful, you may become financially independent. Investments with compound interest grow much faster than those that have simple interest. The younger you are when you start investing, the more your money grows during your working years.

Review Your Knowledge

Circle the correct answer for each of the following.

1. Planning to save enough money to go on a nice vacation is an example of a(n)
    A. need.
    B. investment.
    C. financial goal.
    D. wealth.

2. Which of the following is a need?
    A. Shelter.
    B. Designer clothes.
    C. TV.
    D. Cell phone.

3. A want is
    A. something essential for living.
    B. an expense.
    C. something important to an individual.
    D. something someone would like to have but does not need to live.

4. A value is
    A. something essential for living.
    B. an expense.
    C. a belief about ideas and principles that are important to you.
    D. something you would like to have but do not need to live.

5. Which of the following is the key to becoming financially secure for the average person?
   A. Making a large salary.
   B. Inheriting money.
   C. Working multiple jobs.
   D. Starting to save or invest at an early age.
6. Net worth is the difference between
   A. assets and interest.
   B. liabilities and growth.
   C. assets and liabilities.
   D. growth and investments.
7. Putting money to a use that you hope will increase its value over time is called
   A. net worth.
   B. investing.
   C. average rate of return.
   D. compound interest.
8. The increase in value of your investments over a period of time is called
   A. assets.
   B. liabilities.
   C. financial planning.
   D. growth.
9. The percentage that your savings or other investments earn over a period of time is called
   A. average rate of return.
   B. interest.
   C. compounding.
   D. growth.
10. The amount you place in an investment is called the
    A. interest.
    B. principal.
    C. rate.
    D. time.

For each word or term, write the correct definition using your own words.

11. Financial plan

_____
_____

12. Wants

_____
_____
_____

13. Wealth

_____
_____
_____

14. Net worth

_____
_____
_____

15. Assets

_____
_____
_____

16. Liabilities

_____
_____
_____

17. Financial independence

_____
_____
_____

18. Interest

_____
_____
_____

19. Compound interest

_____
_____
_____

20. Rule of 72

_____
_____
_____

Apply Your Math Skills

Calculate the answers to the following problems.

21. If your assets total $12,365 and your liabilities total $6,924, what is your net worth?

22. The total amount earned on an investment of $3,500 over a period of 10 years is $250. What is the average rate of return?

23. You deposit $1,750 at a rate of 2.5% compounded annually. What amount will you have at the end of 6 years?

24. Your initial deposit is $1,500. The interest is compounded quarterly at 5.25%. You add $250 each quarter for three years. What is the ending balance?

25. Using the Rule of 72, estimate how long it will take to double the above investment at an annual interest rate of 4%.

2 Paychecks: Using Your Money Wisely

Terms

Wage
Gross pay
Time card
Overtime wage
Salary
Deductions
Federal income taxes
Allowances
Social Security
Medicare
State income taxes
Local income taxes
Net pay

Direct deposit
Insurance
Retirement account
Contribution
Benefits

Objectives

When you complete Chapter 2, you will be able to:

- **Calculate** gross earnings, including overtime pay.
- **Calculate** amounts for mandatory deductions.
- **Calculate** amounts for voluntary deductions.
- **Identify** various benefits that employers may offer.

Chapter 2   Paychecks: Using Your Money Wisely

Your Financial IQ

Before you read this chapter, answer the following questions to see how much you already know about paychecks and income taxes.

1. Does your state collect income taxes from wages?

2. If a state does not collect income taxes from wages, how does it get the money it needs to run the state?

3. Would it be advantageous to live in a state that does not collect income taxes? Why or why not?

4. Do you think Social Security taxes should be voluntary? Why or why not?

5. Why are federal income taxes deducted from your paycheck?

6. When you file your taxes at the end of the year, you might get back some or all of the federal and state income taxes deducted from your check. You will not get back any Social Security or Medicare taxes. Why are these taxes not returned to you?

7. List a service provided by federal government tax dollars.

8. List a service provided by state government tax dollars.

9. List a service provided by local government tax dollars.

10. Why should you check to see if your paycheck is calculated correctly?

Calculating Earnings

There is a great feeling about earning that first paycheck. You may already be working part time and have experienced that feeling. All your efforts and hard work to find a job have finally been rewarded! Earning a paycheck is a step toward financial security.

How do you know if your employer has given you the right amount of pay for your work? Do you take for granted that the amount is accurate? This chapter will show you how to verify that the pay you are getting is the correct amount.

Wages

If you are working while you are in school, you are probably being paid an hourly wage. A **wage** is a dollar amount per hour that you get paid for doing work. The total amount of earnings before deductions is called **gross pay.** Gross pay is also known as gross earnings or gross wages. To find gross pay, multiply the hourly wage times the number of hours worked.

$$\text{Hourly Wage} \times \text{Hours Worked} = \text{Gross Pay}$$

> **F.Y.I.** You should always check the math on your paycheck to see if it is calculated correctly. Sometimes mistakes are made.

Example 2-1

A local fast-food establishment offers summer employment paying $7.95 per hour. If you work 23 hours in one week, how much will you earn? (Always round off to the nearest cent.)

Hourly wage	$7.95
Number of hours worked	× 23
Gross pay	$182.85

You do the Math 2-1

You work 17.5 hours in a week. If your wage is $8.85 per hour, what is your gross pay for the week?

Hourly wage	_____
Number of hours worked	_____
Gross pay	_____

Chapter 2 Paychecks: Using Your Money Wisely

Check Your Understanding

What is the formula for calculating gross pay?

_____

_____

Employers must follow U.S. Department of Labor rules when hiring teens. Some states have additional rules that must be followed, as do some industries, such as farming. The basic rules of the Fair Labor Standards Act allow teens who are 14 or 15 years old to work a total of 3 hours per day and 18 hours per week during school weeks. During non-school weeks, these teens can work a total of 8 hours per day and 40 hours per week. The FLSA does not limit the number of hours or times of day for workers 16 years and older.

A **time card** is a record of the time you start work, the time you leave, and any breaks you take. Your employer may require you to fill out a time card, as shown in Figure 2-1. Your company may record this automatically on a time clock. If you work at a company such as a fast food restaurant, you may clock in on your cash register.

Figure 2-1 A Typical Time Card

TIME CARD					
Week Ending	3/6/--		**Name**	Maria Diaz	
Day	**Date**	**Time In**	**Time Out**	**Less Lunch or Break Hours**	**Hours Worked**
Sunday	2/28/--				
Monday	3/1/--	4:00 p.m.	6:45 p.m.	.25	2.5
Tuesday	3/2/--	3:45 p.m.	7:00 p.m.	.25	3.0
Wednesday	3/3/--	4:30 p.m.	6:30 p.m.	0	2.0
Thursday	3/4/--	4:00 p.m.	7:30 p.m.	.5	3.0
Friday	3/5/--	3:45 p.m.	6:30 p.m.	.25	2.5
Saturday	3/6/--	10:30 a.m.	4:00 p.m.	1.00	4.5
Weekly Total Hours					17.5

Time Card

Fill in the following time card and calculate total hours worked. Use the week ended October 16 of the current year.

Monday: Arrive 3:30 p.m., break for 15 minutes at 6:00 p.m., leave at 8:15 p.m.
Thursday: Arrive 4:00 p.m., no break, leave at 7:30 p.m.
Saturday: Arrive 10:00 a.m., lunch break for 30 minutes, afternoon break for 15 minutes, leave at 6:45 p.m.

TIME CARD					
Week Ending			Name		
Day	Date	Time In	Time Out	Less Lunch or Break Hours	Hours Worked
Sunday					
Monday					
Tuesday					
Wednesday					
Thursday					
Friday					
Saturday					
Weekly Total Hours					

Overtime

F.Y.I.
Some jobs pay double the hourly rate for overtime for employees who work on holidays or in other special situations.

Forty hours a week is considered a standard work week. If you work more than 40 hours in a week, you will probably earn overtime wages. An **overtime wage** is the amount paid for working additional hours beyond the standard workweek. The standard overtime hourly wage is 1.5 times the hourly rate.

Hourly Wage × 1.5 = Overtime Hourly Wage

Chapter 2 Paychecks: Using Your Money Wisely

Example 2-2

You earn $8 per hour. What is your overtime wage rate if you work more than 40 hours in one week?

Hourly wage	$8.00
Times 1.5	× 1.5
Hourly overtime wage	$12.00

You Do the Math

You earn $8.35 per hour. What is your overtime wage rate if you work more than 40 hours in one week?

Hourly wage	_____
Times 1.5	_____
Hourly overtime wage	_____

You will add your regular pay for the 40 hours to your overtime pay to get your gross wages for the week.

Example 2-3

Your hourly wage is $8.25. What is your gross pay if you work 43 hours in one week?

Step 1 Calculate your regular earnings.

Hourly wage	$8.25
Regular hours worked	× 40
Regular weekly wages	$330.00

Step 2 Calculate the overtime hourly wage.

Hourly wage	$8.25
Times 1.5	× 1.5
Overtime hourly wage	$12.38

Step 3 Calculate your overtime wages.

Overtime hourly wage	$12.38
Overtime hours	× 3
Overtime wages	$37.14

Step 4 Calculate your gross pay.

Regular earnings	$330.00
Overtime earnings	+ 37.14
Gross pay	$367.14

You Do the Math 2-3

You earn $9.45 per hour. In one week, you work 45 hours. What is your gross pay?

Step 1 Calculate your regular earnings.

    Hourly wage   _____

    Regular hours worked   _____

    Regular weekly wages   _____

Step 2 Calculate the overtime hourly wage.

    Hourly wage   _____

    Times 1.5   _____

    Overtime hourly wage   _____

Step 3 Calculate your overtime wages.

    Overtime rate   _____

    Overtime hours   _____

    Overtime wages   _____

Step 4 Calculate your gross pay.

    Regular earnings   _____

    Overtime earnings   _____

    Gross pay   _____

Check *Your* Understanding

How is gross pay calculated when you have worked more than 40 hours in one week?

_____

_____

_____

_____

Tips

    Employers are required by law to pay workers a certain minimum wage. If you are hired as a server in a restaurant, however, you probably will not receive minimum wage. Servers are typically paid a smaller hourly rate because of the tips they are expected to receive. Many customers add tips to their electronic payments at restaurants instead of leaving cash. The restaurant will then automatically include those tips as part of the server's gross pay for that week.

F.Y.I.
Tips are calculated by the customer based on a percentage of the bill. It is customary to tip 15% to 20% based on the quality of service.

Example 2-4

You are hired as a server in an area restaurant. You make $5.69 per hour plus tips. If you work 18 hours in a week and earn $33.40 in tips, what is your gross pay?

Hourly wage	$5.69
Hours worked	× 18
Wages	$102.42
Tips	+ 33.40
Gross pay	$135.82

You Do the Math 2-4

You work 23 hours in a week as a server in a restaurant. You earn wages of $5.75 per hour and $41.25 in tips. What is your gross pay?

Hourly wage	_____
Hours worked	_____
Wages	_____
Tips	_____
Gross pay	_____

Check Your Understanding

Why do servers generally not receive minimum wage?

_____
_____

Salaries

Employees in some jobs are paid a salary rather than hourly wages. A **salary** is a set amount of money paid to someone in exchange for work. A salary is usually defined as a yearly amount. However, it may be paid weekly, biweekly (every other week), semimonthly (twice a month), or once a month. Some employees who are paid a salary are not paid for any overtime hours that they work. To calculate annual salary, multiply the payment amount by the number of payments per year.

Weekly Salary × 52 Weeks = Annual Salary

Biweekly Salary × 26 = Annual Salary

Semimonthly Salary × 24 = Annual Salary

Monthly Salary × 12 = Annual Salary

Example 2-5

You earn a salary of $600 per week. What are your annual earnings?

Weekly salary	$600.00
Weeks in year	× 52
Annual salary	$31,200.00

You Do the Math 2-5

If you earn a salary of $2,750 per month, what is your annual salary?

Monthly salary	_____
Months in year	_____
Annual salary	_____

Suppose you know the annual salary for a job and you want to calculate how much you will earn per pay period. Divide the annual salary by 12 if you are paid monthly. Divide by 26 if you are paid biweekly. Divide by 24 if you are paid semimonthly or by 52 if you are paid weekly.

Example 2-6

You have been offered a job with an annual salary of $43,750. You will be paid weekly. What will be your gross earnings per week?

Annual salary	$43,750.00
Number of paychecks	÷ 52
Weekly gross pay	$841.35

You Do the Math 2-6

You are offered an annual salary of $51,820. You will be paid biweekly. What will be your gross pay each pay period?

Annual salary	_____
Number of paychecks	_____
Biweekly gross pay	_____

Chapter 2 Paychecks: Using Your Money Wisely

Check Your Understanding

What is the formula for determining monthly or weekly pay if you earn an annual salary?

_____

_____

Wages

1. Visit an online edition of the classified ads from a local newspaper to find various jobs that indicate wages or salaries. List four positions—one that pays weekly, one that pays biweekly, one that pays semimonthly, and one that pays monthly. Calculate annual wages for each position.

Web Connect

Name of Position	Paid	Amount of Pay	Annual Salary
1.	Weekly		
2.	Biweekly		
3.	Semimonthly		
4.	Monthly		

2. List four salaried positions that list annual salaries. Determine weekly, biweekly, semimonthly, and monthly gross pay for each position.

Position	Annual Pay	Weekly	Biweekly	Semimonthly	Monthly
1.					
2.					
3.					
4.					

Calculating Mandatory Deductions

If you have a job, you may be disappointed to see how much is taken out of your check before you receive it. **Deductions** are the amounts subtracted from your gross pay. Some deductions are mandatory (required), such as taxes. Federal income taxes, Social Security taxes, and Medicare taxes are examples.

Federal Income Taxes

A tax is a financial charge or levy that individuals and some organizations pay to fund the services of a government. **Federal income taxes** are taxes on income that are collected by the U.S. government. These taxes are used to provide for national security. They also fund many projects, such as interstate highways and grants for education. The Internal Revenue Service (IRS) provides tax tables for employers. These tables show the amount to be deducted from the employee's pay. Excerpts from these tables are shown in Figure 2-2. (The tables are updated each year, so the ones shown will not be for the current year.)

Figure 2-2 Excerpts from Federal Withholding Tables

SINGLE Persons—WEEKLY Payroll Period
(For Wages Paid Through December 20XX)

And the wages are—		And the number of withholding allowances claimed is—										
At least	But less than	0	1	2	3	4	5	6	7	8	9	10
		The amount of income tax to be withheld is—										
$0	$120	$0	$0	$0	$0	$0	$0	$0	$0	$0	$0	$0
120	125	1	0	0	0	0	0	0	0	0	0	0
125	130	1	0	0	0	0	0	0	0	0	0	0
130	135	2	0	0	0	0	0	0	0	0	0	0
135	140	2	0	0	0	0	0	0	0	0	0	0
140	145	3	0	0	0	0	0	0	0	0	0	0
145	150	3	0	0	0	0	0	0	0	0	0	0
150	155	4	0	0	0	0	0	0	0	0	0	0
155	160	4	0	0	0	0	0	0	0	0	0	0
160	165	5	0	0	0	0	0	0	0	0	0	0
165	170	5	0	0	0	0	0	0	0	0	0	0
170	175	6	0	0	0	0	0	0	0	0	0	0
175	180	6	0	0	0	0	0	0	0	0	0	0
180	185	7	0	0	0	0	0	0	0	0	0	0
185	190	7	0	0	0	0	0	0	0	0	0	0
580	590	66	56	45	35	24	13	5	0	0	0	0
590	600	68	57	47	36	25	15	6	0	0	0	0
600	610	69	59	48	38	27	16	7	0	0	0	0
610	620	71	60	50	39	28	18	8	1	0	0	0
620	630	72	62	51	41	30	19	9	2	0	0	0
630	640	74	63	53	42	31	21	10	3	0	0	0
640	650	75	65	54	44	33	22	12	4	0	0	0
650	660	77	66	56	45	34	24	13	5	0	0	0
660	670	78	68	57	47	36	25	15	6	0	0	0
670	680	80	69	59	48	37	27	16	7	0	0	0

MARRIED Persons—WEEKLY Payroll Period
(For Wages Paid Through December 20XX)

And the wages are—		And the number of withholding allowances claimed is—										
At least	But less than	0	1	2	3	4	5	6	7	8	9	10
		The amount of income tax to be withheld is—										
$0	$270	$0	$0	$0	$0	$0	$0	$0	$0	$0	$0	$0
270	280	1	0	0	0	0	0	0	0	0	0	0
280	290	2	0	0	0	0	0	0	0	0	0	0
290	300	3	0	0	0	0	0	0	0	0	0	0
300	310	4	0	0	0	0	0	0	0	0	0	0
310	320	5	0	0	0	0	0	0	0	0	0	0
320	330	6	0	0	0	0	0	0	0	0	0	0
330	340	7	0	0	0	0	0	0	0	0	0	0
340	350	8	1	0	0	0	0	0	0	0	0	0
350	360	9	2	0	0	0	0	0	0	0	0	0
510	520	27	18	11	4	0	0	0	0	0	0	0
520	530	29	19	12	5	0	0	0	0	0	0	0
530	540	30	20	13	6	0	0	0	0	0	0	0
540	550	32	21	14	7	0	0	0	0	0	0	0
550	560	33	23	15	8	1	0	0	0	0	0	0
560	570	35	24	16	9	2	0	0	0	0	0	0
570	580	36	26	17	10	3	0	0	0	0	0	0
580	590	38	27	18	11	4	0	0	0	0	0	0
590	600	39	29	19	12	5	0	0	0	0	0	0
600	610	41	30	20	13	6	0	0	0	0	0	0

Source: *Publication 15, Employer's Tax Guide*, Department of the Treasury, Internal Revenue Service, www.missouribusiness.net/irs/pdfs/p15.pdf.

Chapter 2 Paychecks: Using Your Money Wisely

The amount deducted from your pay for federal income tax is determined by earnings, marital status, and withholding allowances you claim. **Allowances** are conditions for which you qualify that will lower the amount of income taxes withheld from your pay. For example, people for whom you are financially responsible, such as children, qualify you for an allowance. Allowances are claimed on a Form W-4 tax document as shown in Figure 2-3. You complete this form for your employer. The form has a worksheet that will help you identify allowances. The fewer allowances you claim, the more taxes will be deducted from your pay. Some people claim zero allowances. This allows them to get a larger tax refund when they file their income tax return. As a student, you will probably claim one or zero allowances.

Figure 2-3 Form W-4

Source: Department of the Treasury, Internal Revenue Service, http://www.irs.gov/pub/irs-pdf/fw4.pdf.

Example 2-7

You earn $135 per week at your part time job. You are single and claim zero allowances. How much will be withheld from your paycheck for federal income tax?

- **Step 1** Use the table for single persons (Figure 2-2).

- **Step 2** Find $135. The column heads show "at least $135 but less than $140." Go to the column for zero (0) allowances.

- **Step 3** The amount of tax is $2.

You Do the Math 2-7

Your gross pay is $187.65. You are single and claim zero allowances. How much will be withheld from your paycheck for federal income tax?

Step 1 Use the table for _____ persons.

Step 2 Find $187.65. The column heads show "_____ _____." Go to the column for _____ allowances.

Step 3 The amount of tax is _____.

Check Your Understanding

For what purposes are federal income taxes used?

_____
_____
_____

Federal Income Taxes

1. Using the tax tables that are shown in Figure 2-2, find the withholding for federal income tax for each employee.

Employee Number	Number of Allowances	Marital Status	Gross Pay	Federal Income Tax
1	2	M	$511.70	
2	0	S	581.35	
3	3	M	598.40	
4	5	M	609.00	
5	1	S	675.90	

2. Visit the website for the Internal Revenue Service at www.irs.gov. Search for *tax tables*. Record the income tax for each employee's weekly gross pay using the tax tables for the current year.

Employee Number	Number of Allowances	Marital Status	Gross Pay	Federal Income Tax
1	2	M	$511.70	
2	0	S	581.35	
3	3	M	508.40	
4	5	M	609.00	
5	1	S	675.90	

Social Security Taxes

Social Security is a social insurance program run by the U.S. government. It provides benefits for retired workers, the disabled, and other qualified persons. It was created under the Federal Insurance Contribution Act (FICA). Taxes collected to fund this program are known as Social Security taxes or FICA taxes. You will begin paying these taxes when you start working. Under the current rules, you will be able to collect some benefits when you are age 62. You must be older to

F.Y.I.
The first Social Security payment of $22.54 was issued in 1940. The average monthly benefit in 2010 was around $1,170 per month.

The money that you contribute to Social Security today will help fund your retirement in the future.

Shutterstock

collect full benefits. The age for full benefits varies depending on your date of birth. However, the rules can change. You can find current information on the Social Security website.

Social Security is calculated as a percentage of your pay, currently 6.2% of your gross pay up to $106,800. The limit will most likely change as you get older, and the contribution rate may also increase.

$$\text{Gross Pay} \times \text{Tax Rate} = \text{Social Security Tax}$$

Example 2-8

On your gross earnings of $135, how much will be withheld for Social Security?

Gross pay	$135.00
Social Security tax rate	× .062
Social Security tax withheld	$8.37

You Do the Math 2-8

How much will be withheld for Social Security on earnings of $187.65?

Gross pay	_____
Social Security tax rate	_____
Social Security tax withheld	_____

F.Y.I. Your employer pays Social Security taxes for you equal to the amount you pay.

Check Your Understanding

Why are Social Security taxes deducted from your paycheck?

_____
_____
_____
_____

Medicare Taxes

Another required tax is for Medicare. **Medicare** is a national health insurance program run by the U.S. government. Medicare taxes are collected on income to fund the program. The fund is used to give benefits to those who collect Social Security and meet age and other requirements. Currently,

1.45% of your paycheck is deducted for Medicare taxes. There is no limit on wages that are taxed for Medicare. There will likely be some changes in the tax rate and the program during your lifetime.

$$\text{Gross Pay} \times \text{Tax Rate} = \text{Medicare Tax}$$

As with Social Security, your employer pays Medicare taxes for you equal to the amount you pay.

Example 2-9

On your gross earnings of $135, how much will be deducted for Medicare tax?

Gross pay	$135.00
Medicare tax rate	× .0145
Medicare tax withheld	$1.96

You Do the Math 2-9

How much Medicare tax would be withheld from your gross pay of $187.65?

Gross pay	_____
Medicare tax rate	_____
Medicare tax withheld	_____

Check Your Understanding

What are Medicare taxes used for?

_____

_____

State Income Taxes

State income taxes are taxes on income that are collected by a state government. Most states collect state income taxes. The taxes are used to pay for state services such as state government, roads, education, and other services. As with federal taxes, employers may use a tax table to determine the amount of state taxes to withhold for employees. These tables vary by state. In the following examples, a percentage is used to calculate state taxes.

$$\text{Gross Pay} \times \text{Tax Rate} = \text{State Income Tax}$$

Example 2-10

You have gross earnings of $135. Your state income tax rate is 3%. How much will be withheld for state taxes?

Gross pay	$135.00
State income tax rate	× .03
State income tax withheld	$4.05

You Do the Math 2-10

Your gross pay is $187.65. Your state income tax rate is 6%. How much will be withheld for state tax?

Gross pay	_____
State income tax rate	_____
State income tax withheld	_____

F.Y.I. When you file your yearly tax returns, you may get back some (or all) of the amounts withheld from your pay for federal and state tax. You will not, however, receive any refunds for Social Security or Medicare taxes.

Check Your Understanding

For what purposes are state income taxes used?

_____

_____

State Income Tax Rates

1. Visit websites of various states to determine if the state collects income taxes. List at least five states that *do not* collect state income taxes.

	State
1.	
2.	
3.	
4.	
5.	

2. Find five states that *do* collect state income taxes. List the rate of income taxes collected by these five states.

	State	Tax Rate
1.		
2.		
3.		
4.		
5.		

Local Income Taxes

Local income taxes are taxes paid to a local government, such as a county or city. Local taxes are used for police departments, schools, county or city roads, and other local services. These taxes are also percentages of your pay. Typical amounts are from 0.5% to 2% of gross pay.

Gross Pay × Tax Rate = Local Income Tax

Example 2-11

Your gross pay is $135. The local income tax rate is 1.5%. How much will be withheld for local tax?

Gross pay	$135.00
Local income tax rate	× .015
Local income tax withheld	$2.03

You Do the Math 2-11

Your gross pay is $187.65. The local tax rate is 0.75%. How much will be withheld for local tax?

Gross pay _____

Local income tax rate _____

Local income tax withheld _____

Check Your Understanding

For what purposes are local income taxes used?

_____
_____
_____

Net Pay

Net pay is gross pay minus all deductions. This is the amount you get to keep or actually take home. Therefore, net pay is sometimes called *take home pay*.

Gross Pay – Total Deductions = Net Pay

Example 2-12

This example shows how to calculate the net pay using deductions from the previous examples.

Gross pay		$135.00
Federal income tax	$2.00	
Social Security tax	8.37	
Medicare tax	1.96	
State income tax	4.05	
Local income tax	2.03	
Total deductions		– 18.41
Net pay		$116.59

You Do the Math 2-12

Using your calculations from previous examples, calculate net pay for $187.65.

Gross pay	_____
Federal income tax	_____
Social Security tax	_____
Medicare tax	_____
State income tax	_____
Local income tax	_____
Total deductions	_____
Net pay	_____

Check Your Understanding

How is net pay calculated?

_____

_____

You should receive a paycheck stub that shows your gross pay, all deductions, and net pay. The paycheck stub may show year-to-date figures as well. A sample paycheck stub is shown in Figure 2-4. Keep in mind that if you collect tips, those tips are added to gross pay and, therefore, subject to all taxes. A paycheck stub should also show any voluntary deductions that you elect to have taken from your pay. You will learn about voluntary deductions in the next section.

Your employer may ask if you want to use direct deposit for your pay. **Direct deposit** is a transfer of money (in this case, your net pay) to a checking or savings account. You would receive a payment record similar to a paycheck stub but not a check. Some employers require you to use direct deposit.

F.Y.I.
Unemployment taxes are paid by employers to help provide benefits for workers who are laid off. You should never have a deduction from your paycheck for unemployment taxes.

Dollars and $ense

Using Direct Deposit

As you learned earlier, direct deposit is a transfer of money to your checking or savings account. Many employers require you to use direct deposit. Some government payments, such as for Social Security, are also made by direct deposit.

Why Use Direct Deposit?

❑ By using direct deposit, employers save time and money by not having to issue individual paper checks.

❑ Direct deposit speeds up the process of getting your money into your account. The money will be credited to your account when your employer issues the deposit, thus allowing you quicker access to your cash.

❑ If you do not have the paper check in your hands, you avoid the risk of losing it or having it stolen before you get to the bank.

❑ You save time by not having to go to the bank to deposit your money.

❑ Direct deposit also helps the environment. No checks are written; so paper is saved. You do not have to drive to the bank to deposit your check; so you save the cost of gas.

How Do You Set Up Direct Deposit?

The process for setting up direct deposit is easy. Check with your employer who will provide you a form to complete with your banking information. You will attach a voided check that will show your account number and the bank's routing number. It's that easy!

Figure 2-4 A paycheck stub shows gross pay, deductions, and net pay.

Employee:	Joe Park 225 West Second Street Frankfort, KY 40601-0225		Date: 6/24/--	Jake's Skateboards 82 Hudson Hollow Road Frankfort, KY 40601-0082	
Gross Pay $345.00	Fed. Income Tax Withheld $18.06	State Income Tax Withheld $13.80	FICA Tax Withheld $21.39	Medicare Tax Withheld $5.00	Net Pay $286.75
Gross Pay Year-to-Date $8,484.50	Federal Year-to-Date $444.16	State Year-to-Date $339.38	FICA Year-to-Date $526.04	Medicare Year-to-Date $123.03	Net Pay Year-to-Date $7,051.89

Calculating Voluntary Deductions

You may request that additional deductions be withheld from your paycheck. Some of these might be for health, life, or disability insurance; retirement accounts or other savings plans; or charitable contributions. These deductions may be a set amount or a percentage of your gross pay.

Insurance

Insurance is protection against loss that may occur in certain situations. For example, your home or other property may be damaged in a fire. Property insurance covers this type of loss. Health insurance pays part or all of the costs of medical bills when you have an illness or injury. Your employer may pay for part of your health insurance if you agree to pay the remainder. Your part of the insurance cost would be deducted from your gross pay. Other types of insurance may also be deducted from your gross pay if you choose. These may include life insurance, dental or vision insurance, and disability insurance. Chapter 6 will cover various types of insurance.

If you can get health insurance through your employer, it is probably a good idea to take advantage of this opportunity. You generally will get a better policy at a lower cost with a group than you could on your own.

Savings or Retirement Accounts

Another voluntary deduction may be for a savings or retirement account. A **retirement account** is a savings account specifically set up for your later years when you decide you do not want to work full time. Money can be deducted from your paycheck and put into these accounts. These accounts are discussed in Chapter 10.

> **F.Y.I.**
> Voluntary deductions should be deducted from gross pay only if the employee agrees in writing to have those deductions.

Contributions

You may choose to donate money to a charity or other worthy cause. Money that you donate is called a **contribution** or a donation. Your employer may collect and forward donations for selected organizations. If you choose to make regular donations, that amount would be deducted from your paycheck and sent to that organization. You can use online charity rating sites to learn about charities.

Example 2-13

Your weekly gross pay is $617.85. You elect to put 10% of your gross pay into your retirement account. You also elect to give $5 per pay period to a charity. Your portion of the cost for health insurance is $23 per pay period. What is the total cost of these deductions?

Gross pay	$617.85
Rate for retirement account	× .10
Retirement deduction	$61.79
Retirement deduction	$61.79
Contribution to charity	5.00
Health insurance	+ 23.00
Total voluntary deductions	$89.79

You Do the Math 2-13

Your monthly gross pay is $1,762.35. You elect to have 8% put into a retirement account. You also elect to give $25 per pay period to a charity. Your portion of the cost for health insurance is $117.85 per check. What is the total of these deductions?

Gross pay	_____
Rate for retirement account	_____
Retirement deduction	_____
Retirement deduction	_____
Contribution to charity	_____
Health insurance	_____
Total voluntary deductions	_____

Check Your Understanding

Explain voluntary deductions and give several examples.

_____

_____

Give It a Go

Calculating Net Pay

1. Create a spreadsheet to calculate the weekly payroll for three employees. Use the following terms as the column headings in the spreadsheet.

Column	Heading	Column	Heading	Column	Heading
A	Employee Number	G	Overtime Hourly Wage	M	Social Security Tax
B	Marital Status	H	Overtime Hours	N	Medicare Tax
C	Allowances	I	Overtime Pay	O	Retirement
D	Hourly Wage	J	Gross Pay	P	Health Insurance
E	Regular Hours	K	Federal Income Tax	Q	Total Deductions
F	Regular Pay	L	State Income Tax	R	Net Pay

2. Using the information that follows, enter the employee number, the marital status, and the number of allowances for each employee.

Employee Number	Marital Status	Allowances
1	M	1
2	S	0
3	S	1

3. Using the information that follows, enter the hourly wage, the regular hours, and the overtime hours for each employee. Any hours worked over 40 are overtime hours. Enter a formula to calculate the regular pay.

Employee Number	Total Hours Worked	Hourly Wage
1	42	$12.50
2	19	8.50
3	47	11.65

4. The overtime hourly wage is 1.5 times the hourly wage. Enter a formula to calculate the overtime hourly wage for each employee. Enter a formula to calculate the overtime pay for each employee. Enter a formula to calculate the gross pay for each employee.
5. Use the tax tables shown in Figure 2-2 to find the federal income tax for each employee. Enter the numbers in the spreadsheet.
6. The rate for state income taxes is 5%. Enter a formula to calculate the amount of state income tax for each employee.
7. The rate for Social Security taxes is 6.2%. The rate for Medicare taxes is 1.45%. Enter formulas to calculate the amounts for the Social Security and Medicare taxes for each employee.
8. Employee 1 and Employee 3 have 8% of their gross pay deducted for a retirement account. Enter a formula to calculate this deduction for these two employees.
9. Employee 1 and Employee 2 each have $22.50 deducted for health insurance. Enter these amounts in the spreadsheet.
10. Enter a formula to calculate the total deductions for each employee. Enter a formula to calculate the net pay for each employee.

Benefits

Benefits are services or things of value that employees receive from employers in addition to their pay. Vacation pay, group health insurance, and sick days are examples of benefits. Companies are not required to provide benefits for their workers. Benefits are offered to attract employees and encourage them to stay with the company. At many companies, benefits are offered only to full-time employees. Sometimes benefits may be worth more than an increase in pay if they are not taxable.

Benefits are also called fringe benefits.

Vacation Pay

Company policy may allow you to have one week of paid vacation after the first year. The amount of vacation time may increase as you build your service with the company. All companies are different. You should check with the Human Resources department of your company for specific information. One week of vacation is five days. Some companies may allow you to accumulate vacation time. In other words, whatever vacation time you do not use in one year, you may take in later years.

If you are a full-time employee, you will probably be paid for holidays. However, you usually have to work the day before and/or the day after the holiday to be eligible for holiday pay.

Sick Days

Company policies vary widely in offering paid sick days. Some companies do not pay at all if you are sick. Others pay only if the employee is sick (and not a member of the employee's family). Other companies may have a set number of sick days you may use each year when you or a family member is ill. Some companies will require you to have a doctor's excuse, while others may just have you sign a statement that states that you or a family member was ill. As with paid vacation days, the number of sick days may vary depending on how long you have been with the company. Once you have used all your sick days, you are not paid, even if you have to be in the hospital with a serious illness.

Personal Days

Personal days can usually be used for any reason. If you decide you want to take the day off so you can chaperone a class field trip at your child's school, you would use a personal day. You will typically get only one or two days per year for paid personal days. Personal days may sometimes be granted to only a few employees at a time.

Emergency Days

Emergency days may be limited to one or two days per year and probably will not carry forward to the next year if unused. They may be used for serious situations that require you to be away from work. For example, your car might break down on your way to work, requiring you to be absent from work.

Bereavement Days

Bereavement days are used for time off from work when a close family member dies. A spouse, child, sibling, grandparent, aunt, uncle, or those relatives by marriage are examples of people who are considered close relatives. You may get up to three bereavement days per year. These days do not typically carry forward if unused.

Why do employers give benefits to their employees?

_____

_____

**Verify Your Paycheck
A Checklist**

When you start working, it is up to you to make sure you are being paid the correct amount and that your deductions are accurate. If you are currently employed, review your latest paycheck stub using this checklist. It is especially important to review the first paycheck with a new employer or after a change in pay.

Yes	No	
___	___	1. Name—is it spelled correctly?
___	___	2. Address—is it accurate?
___	___	3. Employee number—is it accurate?
___	___	4. Is the time period recorded correctly?
___	___	5. Withholdings—does the amount for taxes seem reasonable considering the number of exemptions I selected?
___	___	6. Number of hours—did I get paid for the correct number of hours that I worked?
___	___	7. Calculations—check the math. Is the net pay correct?
___	___	8. Deductions—did I elect to have any voluntary deductions? If so, are they accurate?
___	___	9. Are the year-to-date earnings correct?
___	___	10. If my check should be direct deposited, is it noted accurately on the payment record?

Chapter Review

Summary

The satisfaction you get from earning a paycheck is a great feeling! You should check to be sure that your pay has been calculated correctly. Federal income taxes, Social Security taxes, and Medicare taxes should be deducted from your gross pay. State and local governments may also have income taxes. If so, these taxes will also be deducted. Some companies allow voluntary deductions. These amounts may be for things such as insurance or a retirement plan. Benefits, such as paid vacation and sick days, are offered by some companies to help attract and keep workers. These benefits may not be available to you until you are working full-time.

Review Your Knowledge

Circle the correct answer for each of the following.

1. Most businesses pay overtime after you have worked how many regular hours in a week?
   A. 30
   B. 35
   C. 40
   D. 45
2. When you need to miss work to go to your grandmother's funeral, you would use
   A. sick days.
   B. emergency days.
   C. vacation days.
   D. bereavement days.
3. If you want to take a day off from work to see your sister in a school play, you would use a(n)
   A. sick day.
   B. personal day.
   C. bereavement day.
   D. emergency day.

4. Which of the following is *not* considered a benefit?
   A. Overtime pay.
   B. Vacation pay.
   C. Sick days.
   D. Personal days.

5. Which of the following is *not* a mandatory deduction?
   A. Federal income tax.
   B. Social Security tax.
   C. Medicare tax.
   D. Charitable contribution.

6. Net pay also known as
   A. overtime pay.
   B. take home pay.
   C. Social Security wages.
   D. Medicare wages.

7. A national retirement account for most workers is
   A. Social Security.
   B. Medicare.
   C. vacation pay.
   D. personal leave.

8. Mandatory deductions from pay
   A. include only federal and state income taxes.
   B. are for charitable contributions.
   C. are required deductions.
   D. are only for full-time employees.

9. Which of the following is matched by the employer?
   A. State income tax.
   B. Medicare tax.
   C. Federal income tax.
   D. Net pay.

10. Which of the following taxes are paid only by the employer?
    A. Social Security tax.
    B. Medicare tax.
    C. Federal income tax.
    D. Unemployment tax.

For each word or term, write the correct definition using your own words.

11. Wage

12. Time card

13. Gross pay

14. Overtime wage

15. Salary

16. Deduction

17. Social Security

18. Medicare

19. Net pay

20. Benefits

Apply Your Math Skills

Calculate the answers to the following problems.

21. You earn $8.40 per hour and work 31 hours. What is your gross pay?

22. Your wages are $9.35 per hour. What is your overtime wage per hour?

23. You earn $9.55 per hour and work 46 hours in a week. What is your gross pay?

24. You earn $6.30 per hour plus tips. If you work 26 hours this week and collect $26.35 in tips, what is your gross pay?

25. If your biweekly gross pay is $979.35, what is your annual salary?

26. You apply for a position that pays $39,640 annually. What would be your gross pay per week?

27. Your gross pay is $164.24. You are single and claim zero allowances. How much will be withheld for federal taxes? Use the tables shown in Figure 2-2.

28. Your gross pay is $568.93. How much is withheld for Social Security taxes?

29. Your gross pay is $683.47. How much is withheld for Medicare taxes?

30. Your state tax rate is 6%. How much will be withheld if your gross pay is $721.52?

31. The county where you live has a local tax rate of 1.75%. How much would be withheld if your gross pay is $311.89?

32. Your gross pay is $592.50. You are married and claim one allowance. In addition to federal income taxes, Social Security taxes, and Medicare taxes, your employer deducts 4% for state income tax. What is your net pay?

33. Your gross pay is $327.68. You want your employer to deduct 8 percent of gross pay for your retirement account and $27 for a charitable contribution. What are your total voluntary deductions?

34. You earn $8.75 per hour and your friend earns $8.40 per hour. If you both work 22 hours this week, how much more will you earn?

35. You are offered a health insurance plan through your company. The total cost per month is $465. You are required to pay 1/4 of the cost. How much will be deducted from your check for health insurance?

3 Budgeting: Keeping Track of Your Money

Terms

Budget
Expenses
Fixed expenses
Variable expenses
Income
Discretionary income

Objectives

When you complete Chapter 3, you will be able to:

- **Explain** the purpose of a budget.
- **Identify and calculate** fixed and variable expenses.
- **Calculate** average monthly income and discretionary income.
- **Create** a monthly budget.

Chapter 3 Budgeting: Keeping Track of Your Money

Your Financial IQ

Before you read this chapter, answer the following questions to see how much you already know about budgeting.

1. What is a budget?

2. How do you think using a budget could help you manage your money?

3. What does it mean to "pay yourself first" when managing your money?

4. How do you keep track of how much money you spend in a typical day?

5. What is a fixed expense?

6. What is a variable expense?

7. What is discretionary income?

8. Is a budget necessary if you have a high income?

9. What does it mean to have a surplus?

10. What does it mean to have a deficit?

Budgets

In Chapter 1, you learned some of the basics of financial planning. The next step you will take toward your financial plan is to create a budget. What is a budget? A **budget** is an estimate (usually by category) of expected income and expenses for a given period of time. A budget may be prepared for a week, a month, or a longer period, such as a year. A budget is a useful tool that can help you keep track of your money and spend wisely.

In Chapter 1, you set short-term and long-term goals. These goals were based first on your values, then on your needs and wants. These goals will help you as you create your budget. Go back to Chapter 1 and take a look at the goals you set. Review these goals before you move forward with the next section. Make sure these goals are appropriate for you so that you can use them to create your budget.

Budgeting
A Checklist

Do you ever wonder where your money goes? Do you get to the end of the week and find that you no longer have any money to spend? It is important to keep track of money you have and what you spend to be financially responsible.

Yes	No	
____	____	1. Did I spend my weekly budget on needs?
____	____	2. Did I spend my weekly budget on wants?
____	____	3. Did I have money left over this week to put in savings?
____	____	4. Did I write down everything that I spent money on?
____	____	5. Did I resist buying something that I really didn't need?
____	____	6. Did I run out of money this week?
____	____	7. Did I have to borrow money to make it through the week?
____	____	8. Did I learn anything this week about my spending and savings habits?
____	____	9. Did I buy something this week that I regret?
____	____	10. Was there something I really wanted to buy this week that I did not have enough money to buy?

Chapter 3   Budgeting: Keeping Track of Your Money

Check *Your* Understanding

What is the purpose of a budget?

_____

_____

Expenses

Expenses are amounts paid for goods or services. Do you pay for your school lunches? Your clothes? Your cell phone? Entertainment? These are examples of expenses.

Expenses are categorized as either fixed or variable. **Fixed expenses** are those that stay the same each month, such as amounts paid for school lunches or bus passes. **Variable expenses** are those that change from month to month, such as amounts paid for cell phones bills or spending for personal care items.

As a teen, you probably do not have many expenses beyond those for your personal needs. However, as you graduate and go to college or your first full-time job, you will find there are a lot more expenses to consider. Items such as rent, utilities, groceries, and many other expenses will need to be tracked. Getting in the habit of tracking your spending now will help make it easier when your expenses are greater.

F.Y.I.

Examples of fixed expenses for adults would be mortgage or rent payments and car payments.

Having a cell phone is a variable expense that should be included in your budget each month.

Shutterstock

Categorizing Expenses

Expenses can be fixed or variable. Think about the expenses listed in the table below. Decide whether each expense would be fixed or variable. Put an X in the appropriate column for each expense in the table.

Expense	Fixed	Variable
Cell phone		
DVD rentals		
Music downloads		
Gas for the car		
Car insurance		
Movie tickets		
School lunches		
Bus pass for school		
Gifts		
Clothes		
Eating out with friends		
Other entertainment		
Sports clothing/equipment		
Haircuts		
Monthly dues at local gym		

Do you know where your money goes? If you are like many others, you spend it but do not always remember what you spent it for. If you want to build wealth and have a solid financial plan, you must start paying attention to how you spend your money. The best way to start is to create a daily record of what you spend. If you track your spending for several weeks, you will get an idea of how much you should plan for expenses in your budget.

Chapter 3 Budgeting: Keeping Track of Your Money

Example 3-1

To create a weekly spending record, write the amounts you spend for fixed and variable expenses each day. Then total the amounts for each day and for the week. The weekly spending record for Carlos Acosta is shown below.

Weekly Spending Record
Carlos Acosta
For the week of September 10, 20--

Amounts Spent

	Day 1	Day 2	Day 3	Day 4	Day 5	Day 6	Day 7	Total
Fixed Expenses								
School lunches	$2.75	$2.75	$2.75	$2.75	$2.75			$13.75
Bus fare to work		1.35		1.35		$1.35		4.05
Savings deposit	20.00							20.00
Total Fixed Expenses	22.75	4.10	2.75	4.10	2.75	1.35		37.80
Variable Expenses								
Birthday gift for sister			5.50					5.50
School music fee				22.00				22.00
New music CD		8.95						8.95
Lunch with friends					11.45			11.45
New T-shirt							7.29	7.29
Total Variable Expenses		8.95	5.50	22.00	11.45		7.29	55.19
Total Expenses	$22.75	$13.05	$8.25	$26.10	$14.20	$1.35	$7.29	$92.99

You Do the Math 3-1

The weekly spending record for Carlos Acosta for the week ending September 17 is shown below. How much has Carlos spent for the week? Total the amounts for each day and for the week.

	Day 1	Day 2	Day 3	Day 4	Day 5	Day 6	Day 7	Total
Weekly Spending Record — Carlos Acosta — For the week of September 17, 20--								
Amounts Spent								
Fixed Expenses								
School lunches	$2.75	$2.75	$2.75	$2.75	$2.75			
Bus fare to work		1.35	1.35	1.35				
Savings deposit	15.00							
Total Fixed Expenses	17.75	4.10	4.10	4.10	2.75			
Variable Expenses								
School workbook		18.95						
New music CD			10.85					
Lunch with friends					10.00			
New clothes						35.49		
Total Variable Expenses		18.95	10.85		10.00	35.49		
Total Expenses								

Check Your Understanding

Are most of your expenses fixed or variable? Give two examples of variable expenses that you may have during a month.

_____

_____

Chapter 3 Budgeting: Keeping Track of Your Money

Tracking Your Spending

It is important to keep track of how you spend your money. Record your expenses from last week in this chart. You will need to write the categories for your expenses. Then total the amounts for each day and for the week.

Weekly Spending Record

Name: _____

For the Week Ending: _____

	Amounts Spent							
	Day 1	Day 2	Day 3	Day 4	Day 5	Day 6	Day 7	Total
Fixed Expenses								
Variable Expenses								
Total Expenses								

Income

In planning a budget, an important step is to estimate what your income will be. **Income** is money you receive. Pay from a job, a birthday gift, and an allowance are examples of income. In the following examples, you will work with a monthly budget and monthly income amounts.

Average Monthly Income

Pay from a job is a major source of income for many people. Your net pay may not be the same every week or every month. If you have a part-time job, you may work a different number of days or hours each week. If you have a full-time job, you might sometimes be sick and not work a full week. To create a monthly budget, you will need to calculate your average monthly net pay. To find average monthly net pay, divide the total net pay by the number of months.

Total Net Pay ÷ Number of Months = Average Monthly Net Pay

Example 3-2

You receive weekly paychecks from your job. Your paychecks for three months were for the amounts shown below. What is your average monthly net pay for this time period?

Month	Net Pay Amounts	Totals
May	$98.00	
	75.50	
	125.50	
	<u>145.50</u>	
		$444.00
June	165.75	
	190.60	
	98.00	
	<u>201.35</u>	
		655.70
July	125.50	
	165.75	
	98.00	
	<u>118.75</u>	
		<u>508.00</u>
Total Net Pay		$1,607.70
Number of Months		÷ 3
Average Monthly Net Pay		$535.90

Chapter 3 Budgeting: Keeping Track of Your Money

You Do the Math 3-2

You receive weekly paychecks from your job. Your paychecks for three months were for the amounts shown below. What is your average monthly net pay for this time period?

Month	Net Pay Amounts	Totals
May	$108.00	
	125.00	
	79.00	
	135.50	
		_____
June	122.50	
	100.50	
	135.75	
	75.50	
		_____
July	98.00	
	56.50	
	126.75	
	130.00	
		_____
Total Net Pay		_____
Number of Months		_____
Average Monthly Net Pay		_____

You may not have a regular weekly job during the school year. Thus, your income may vary and come from many different sources. After you have calculated your net pay, you can record your total income using a table similar to the one shown in Figure 3-1.

As a teen, your income is probably not very high. However, after you graduate and have a career, your income should increase. Learning to manage your income now will help you as you make more money in the future.

Figure 3-1 Carlos kept track of his income for a month using this table.

Monthly Income
Carlos Acosta
For the Month of September, 20--

Source	Amount
Pay	
Part-time job	$368.42
Babysitting	15.00
Yard work for neighbors	45.00
Allowance	40.00
Gifts	25.00
Total Income	**$493.42**

Tracking Your Income

Review your income from last month and record the numbers in this chart. Write categories for your income in the first column and amounts in the second column. Total the Amount column.

Monthly Income

Name:	
For the Month of:	
Source	**Amount**
Total Income	**$**

Discretionary Income

After you total your expenses and subtract from your income, hopefully you will have money left over. This extra money is called discretionary income. **Discretionary income** is money that remains after you have paid for regular or needed expenses. This is money that you can put in savings or use for leisure or other activities. It is also called disposable income. If you do not track your income and expenses using a budget, you may find that you have no discretionary income. To calculate discretionary income, subtract your total fixed and variable expenses from your income.

Income − Fixed and Variable Expenses = Discretionary Income

> **F.Y.I.**
> Money that remains after expenses are paid is also referred to as a surplus. When there is not enough income to pay all expenses, this is called a deficit. You may recognize the terms surplus and deficit from when government spending is discussed on TV.

Example 3-3

In Example 3-1, you learned how to calculate weekly expenses. In the first example, the weekly expense total for Carlos Acosta was $92.99. Suppose Carlos spends this much every week. Will he have enough money to cover his expenses based on his September income as shown in Figure 3-1? What will be the amount of his discretionary income?

Weekly spending	$92.99
Number of weeks	× 4
Total monthly expenses	$371.96
Monthly income	$493.42
Monthly expenses	− 371.96
Discretionary income	$121.46

You Do the Math 3-3

In the You Do the Math 3-1 activity, you found the weekly expenses for Carlos. If Carlos spends this much every week, will he have enough money to cover his expenses based on his September income as shown in Figure 3-1? What will be the amount of his discretionary income?

Weekly spending	_____
Number of weeks	_____
Total monthly expenses	_____
Monthly income	_____
Monthly expenses	_____
Discretionary income	_____

Creating a Budget

After you have tracked your spending for a few weeks, you will see a pattern. This pattern of spending will help you decide how much you need for movies, lunch, and other items that you purchase during the week. Once you have an idea of how much you need for specific items, you are ready to create your budget. A budget will remind you how much you want to spend each week.

To create a budget:

- Select a time period for the budget, such as one month.
- List the amounts of income for the period and total them.
- List the fixed and variable expenses for the time period and total them.
- Subtract the total expenses from the total income to find discretionary income.
- If the discretionary income amount is a negative number, reduce expenses.

Remember that as your income and expenses change, so will your budget. A budget is a working document. You will want to review it often. There is no set format for a budget. The one in Figure 3-2 shows a budget for a typical teen.

Creating a Budget

1. Using your information for income and expenses, create a budget for one month. Use a spreadsheet program (or write the information on paper if you do not have access to a spreadsheet). Refer to Figure 3-2 for the column headings, labels, and types of information you should enter.
2. Save the budget file on the hard drive or other storage as directed by your teacher. Use a unique name for your file. For example, if your name is Chad Parker, save the file as C Parker Nov Budget. Each month you will be able to update the budget amounts as needed.

Now that you have completed your budget, you have taken a big step in planning for your future. By keeping track of your income and planning what you will spend, you will have some control over your finances.

Have you heard the saying "pay yourself first"? This saying means that you should budget for savings before you budget for spending. If you do not plan to save money in your budget, you probably will not have money left over to save. Follow the tips in Figure 3-3 to help you stick with your budget.

Chapter 3   Budgeting: Keeping Track of Your Money

Figure 3-2   Budget for Carlos Acosta

Carlos Acosta
Budget
For the Month of June, 20--

Income			
Pay from part-time job	$268.42		
Babysitting	25.00		
Yard work for neighbors	50.00		
Allowance	30.00		
Gifts	<u>25.00</u>		
Total Income			$398.42
Expenses			
Fixed Expenses			
Savings	100.00		
Bus fare to work	16.20		
School lunches	<u>55.00</u>		
Total Fixed Expenses		171.20	
Variable Expenses			
Miscellaneous	40.00		
School fees	18.00		
Entertainment	40.00		
Clothing	50.00		
Eating out with friends	<u>45.00</u>		
Total Variable Expenses		<u>193.00</u>	
Total Expenses			<u>364.20</u>
Discretionary Income			$34.22

Why is it important to create a budget? How will a budget help you in creating a financial plan?

_____
_____
_____
_____

Figure 3-3 Resolve to follow your budget.

Tips for Budgeting

- Keep track of the amounts you spend each week.
- Transfer that information to a budget each month.
- Pay yourself first.
- Be disciplined.
- Stay organized.
- Review the budget regularly.
- Make changes when necessary.

Budgeting Software

1. Do a search for budgeting software on the Internet. Try to find five different programs and record them in the table that follows.

	Name of Software	Cost
1.		
2.		
3.		
4.		
5		

2. If your teacher permits, download a free budgeting software program and create your budget. Was the software easy to use?

_____

Dollars and $ense

Budgeting

Budgeting is an important step toward financial planning. It will guide your future spending and help you be financially responsible. By learning how to create a budget now, you will be able to make decisions more wisely for saving and spending money in the future.

Being organized is important when creating your budget. If you do not keep receipts and other records, it will be difficult to be accurate when tracking your spending. This means that when you create your monthly budget, you may omit expenses. In that case, your budget would not be accurate.

There are many ways of keeping track of your income and expenses. Here are some things you can do each day or week to prepare for your budget.

- ❑ Each time you spend money, be sure to get a receipt. On the receipt, write the item or service you purchased. Put the receipt in an envelope. At the end of the day, record these receipts on your daily spending chart.
- ❑ When you get your paychecks, put all of your pay stubs in an envelope. If your job is cutting grass, you may be paid in cash. If you receive cash, write how much you receive, the date, and the job on a piece of paper. Put this piece of paper in your envelope.
- ❑ If you take money out of your checking or savings account, put the receipt in your envelope.
- ❑ If you cash your paycheck, divide your money into envelopes for fixed and variable expenses. This will help you avoid overspending on things you do not really need.
- ❑ If you have access to a computer at home, you may want to keep track of this information on a spreadsheet or program specifically created for budgeting.

Chapter Review

Summary

A budget is an estimate of expected income and expenses for a given period of time. A budget may be prepared for a week, a month, or a longer period, such as a year. Expenses are amounts paid for goods or services. Fixed expenses are those that stay the same each month, such as amounts paid for school lunches or bus passes. Variable expenses are those that change from month to month, such as amounts paid for cell phone bills. Income is money you receive, such as pay from a job or an allowance. Money that remains after you have paid for regular or needed expenses is called discretionary income. As your income and expenses change, so will your budget. A budget is a working document that you will want to review often.

Review Your Knowledge

Circle the correct answer for each of the following.

1. You can track your expected income and expenses for a given period using a(n)
   A. financial goal.
   B. investment.
   C. budget.
   D. deficit.

2. You paid $12.50 for a new music CD. This amount represents a(n)
   A. income.
   B. expense.
   C. goal.
   D. charge.

3. Last week, you paid $4.50 for lunch on Monday, $3.00 for lunch on Tuesday, and $2.75 for lunch on the other weekdays. The amounts you paid for lunch are
   A. fixed expenses.
   B. variable expenses.
   C. discretionary expenses.
   D. discretionary income.

4. Money you receive for working at a job is an example of
   A. income.
   B. an expense.
   C. discretionary income.
   D. a financial goal.

5. The phrase "pay yourself first" means that you should
   A. set aside money for all your wants in your budget.
   B. write yourself a check for spending money every week.
   C. set aside money to save as part of your budget.
   D. None of the above.

Build Your Vocabulary

For each word or term, write the correct definition using your own words.

6. Budget

7. Fixed expenses

8. Variable expenses

9. Income

10. Discretionary income

Apply Your Math Skills

Calculate the answers to the following problems.

11. The weekly spending record for Alice Wong for the week ending October 7 is shown below. How much has Alice spent for the week? Total the amounts for each day and for the week.

	Weekly Spending Record Alice Wong For the week of October 7, 20--							
	Amounts Spent							
	Day 1	Day 2	Day 3	Day 4	Day 5	Day 6	Day 7	Total
Fixed expenses								
School lunches	$3.00	$3.00	$3.00	$3.00	$3.00			
Bus fare	0.50	1.25	1.35	0.75	0.50			
Savings deposit			25.00					
Total fixed expenses	$3.50	$4.25	$29.35	$3.75	$3.50			
Variable expenses								
School supplies or fees	12.50		4.50		2.25			
E-book purchases		1.50		7.75				
Meals with friends			5.50			8.75	6.75	
Clothes and shoes					6.30	25.89		
Total variable expenses	12.50	1.50	10.00	7.75	8.55	34.64	6.75	
Total expenses								

12. You receive weekly paychecks from your job. Your paychecks for three months were for the amounts shown below. What is your average monthly net pay for this time period?

Month	Net Pay Amounts	Totals
June	$175.50	
	125.00	
	110.50	
	135.50	
		_____
July	100.50	
	75.50	
	135.75	
	150.75	
		_____
August	135.00	
	50.75	
	128.50	
	130.00	
		_____
Total net pay		_____
Number of months		_____
Average monthly net pay		_____

13. Latoya's monthly income is $325. Her expenses for a typical week are $75. If Latoya spends this much each week during the month, will she have enough money to cover her expenses? What will be the amount of her discretionary income?

Weekly spending   _____

Number of weeks   _____

Total monthly expenses   _____

Monthly income   _____

Monthly expenses   _____

Discretionary income   _____

14. After you graduate and get a full-time job, your earnings and expenses will increase. Suppose you have the income and expenses listed below. How much will you have for discretionary income?

Monthly Income and Expenses	
Net pay	$3,000.00
Savings	12% of net pay
Donations to charity	35.00
Rent	455.00
Utilities	98.00
Cable, Internet, and phone services	85.00
Car payment and insurance	480.00
Groceries	235.00
Gas	130.00
College tuition, fees, and books	295.00
Health insurance and personal care	350.00
Payment on a credit card balance	120.00
Clothes	110.00
Miscellaneous expenses	100.00

4 Banking: Managing Your Money

Terms

Checking account
Liquid
Service charge
Check register
Electronic banking
Overdraft
Overdraft protection
Post-dated check
Certificate of deposit
Annual percentage yield (APY)
Money market account

Debit card
ATM
Outstanding check
FDIC
Savings and loan association
Credit union

Objectives

When you complete Chapter 4, you will be able to:

- **Describe** four types of common bank accounts.
- **Describe** debit cards and their uses.
- **Explain** FDIC insurance and what it provides consumers.
- **Describe** the services provided by other financial institutions, such as savings and loan associations and credit unions.

Your Financial IQ

Before you read this chapter, answer the following questions to see how much you already know about banking services.

1. What is the difference between a savings account and a checking account?

2. Do checking and savings accounts pay interest?

3. What is a certificate of deposit (CD) and how is it different from a savings account?

4. What is the difference between a debit card and a credit card?

5. What are the advantages and disadvantages of using a debit card?

6. Explain the term *overdraft*.

7. What does it mean to postdate a check?

8. How would compound interest affect the balances in your checking and savings accounts?

9. What is the FDIC?

10. Explain how a money market account works.

Common Bank Accounts

Most teens are familiar with banks and some of their services. You may already be familiar with many banking services, such as checking or savings accounts. Some of the most common services that banks offer are:

- Checking accounts
- Savings accounts
- Certificates of deposit
- Money market accounts

You should plan to keep some of your money in an insured, no-risk account to be used in emergency situations. Banks offer protection and easy access to your money. Many investments are not risk free, so it is important to keep some money safe and readily available. It is wise to keep at least three to six months' basic living expenses in a money market or other liquid account for emergency expenses.

When you go to the bank to open an account, make sure you take pieces of identification with you. You will also need your Social Security number. The bank will need to verify your identity as you complete the application forms for an account.

Opening a bank account is an important step in financial planning. Your bank accounts will help you manage your money as well as earn interest to grow your money.

Checking Accounts

A **checking account** is a type of bank account that allows you to make deposits, write checks, and withdraw your money at any time. These accounts are sometimes called *put and take accounts*. Another word to describe these accounts is liquid. A **liquid** investment is one that can be bought, sold, or converted to cash quickly. Using a checking account is a convenient, safe way to make payments and keep track of how you spend your money.

When you get ready to open a checking account, be sure to shop around. Some checking accounts pay interest. However, these accounts often require that a minimum balance, such as $500 to $1,000, be kept in the account. Your bank may also offer checking accounts that include electronic banking or automated teller services. Check to see which types of accounts are available and select one that fits your needs.

Some banks have basic or student accounts with minimal or no service charges. A **service charge** is a fee you must pay the bank for having an account. The fee may relate to the number of checks you write during a month. An example of a check is shown in Figure 4-1. If you do not write many checks each month, there may not be a service charge for the account. However, there may be hefty charges if you go over your limit, so keep track of the number of checks you write.

Some banks offer checking accounts with no service charges when you have your paycheck directly deposited into your account. If you go to the bank and deposit your check, you will need to complete a deposit slip. A sample deposit slip is shown in Figure 4-2.

F.Y.I. When you write a check, always use ink. Make sure that every line is complete so that no one can change any information on the check.

Why would you want to have a checking account?

_____

_____

Dollars and $ense

On the Lookout for Identity Theft

Have you heard the term *identity theft*? Identity theft happens when someone uses your personal information without your permission. The identity thief might withdraw money from your bank account or buy items using your credit card number. Identity theft is a serious crime. If you are a victim of this crime, it may cost you a great deal of money. It can also take a lot of time to correct problems with your finances caused by the crime.

Be very careful to protect your identity when using banking services. The bank will require your Social Security number to open an account. However, be careful not to write your social security number on other papers.

Your Social Security number will identify you throughout your life. It is used to identify you for income taxes and various types of accounts. Protect your Social Security number. Do not give your number to anyone on the phone or online unless you are sure of their identity. There are many imposters who say they work for banks or credit card companies. Their online requests look legitimate. However, banks and other institutions should never ask for personal information online.

Here are some guidelines to follow to help protect your identity:

- Always shred or destroy any document that has your Social Security number on it. Do not just toss the documents into the trash.
- When your bank statements arrive, place them in a safe place or shred them.
- Keep your PINs safe. Do not put them in an obvious place where someone can steal them, such as in your wallet or purse.
- The bank will give you a document that explains the privacy policy of the institution. Make sure you read the fine print and ask questions if you do not understand the policy. The bank should not give any personal or financial information about you to anyone without your approval.

Chapter 4 Banking: Managing Your Money

Figure 4-1 All lines on a check should be completed so that the check cannot be altered easily.

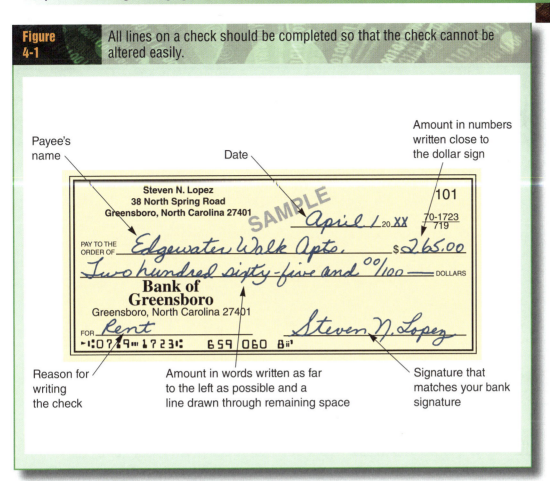

Figure 4-2 A completed deposit slip may look like the one in this example.

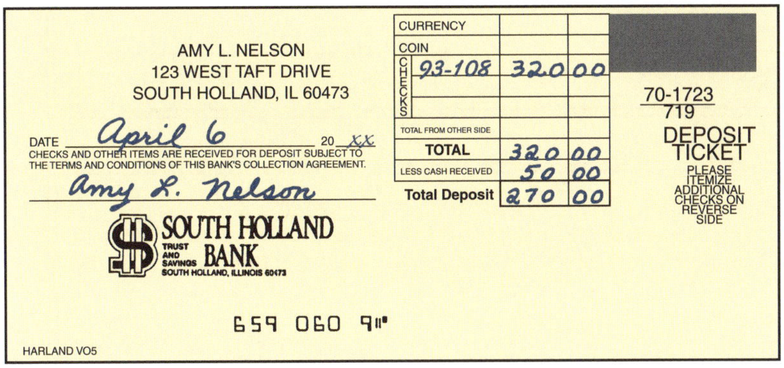

Deposit Slips and Checks

Complete deposit slips and checks for the following transactions. Use the current year in the dates.

Oct. 1:   Deposit check for $128.50
Oct. 4:   Check #104 to City Foods for $32.68 for groceries
Oct. 9:   Check #105 to Dream Music for $9.25 for a music CD
Oct. 17: Deposit cash of $50
Oct. 26: Check #106 for $12.75 to FunLand for games

Main St. Bank

DEPOSIT

Today's Date _____

Customer Name *(Please Print)*
_____

Sign Here *(If cash is received from this deposit)*
X _____

▼ Start your account number here
0 0 0 9 4 2 1 3 0 1 3 6 5 0 | TOTAL $

CASH ▶
CHECK ▶
TOTAL FROM OTHER SIDE ▶
SUBTOTAL ▶
CASH BACK ▶

Student Name
1234 School Street
Anytown, USA 55615

Date _____

Pay to
The Order of _____ $ _____

_____ dollars

Memo _____
Account # 0009-4213-:01-36-50

Student Name
1234 School Street
Anytown, USA 55615

Date _____

Pay to
The Order of _____ $ _____

_____ dollars

Memo _____
Account # 0009-4213-:01-36-50

Chapter 4 Banking: Managing Your Money

Example 4-1

A bank may offer student checking accounts to high school or college students. Students typically write only a few checks per month. Suppose the bank charges a monthly service charge of $9.50 plus $0.32 per check. What will be the total fees if you write six checks in one month?

Step 1 Calculate the charges for the checks

Charge per check	$0.32
Number of checks	× 6
Charges for checks	$1.92

Step 2 Add charges for the checks to the service charge for the month

Monthly service charge	$9.50
Charge for checks	+ $1.92
Total fees	$11.42

You Do the Math 4-1

Your bank charges a monthly service charge of $8.50 plus $0.35 per check. What will be the total fees if you write nine checks in one month?

Step 1 Calculate the charges for the checks

Charge per check _____

Number of checks _____

Charges for checks _____

Step 2 Add charges for the checks to the service charge for the month

Monthly service charge _____

Charges for checks _____

Total fees _____

A **check register** is a record of your checking account transactions. It shows deposits, payments, withdrawals, interest, and fees. It is essential to record every check, withdrawal, and deposit you make so you always know how much you have in your account. Be sure to subtract service charges from your register when you receive your bank statement each month. You will also need to add any interest earned for the month. To keep an accurate check register, you will record your information as shown in Figure 4-3.

Each month, your bank will send you a statement. The statement shows all activity in your checking account for the month. Keep your statements in a safe place where others cannot see them to avoid identity theft. Every month, you should compare your bank statement with your own records and complete a bank reconciliation. A sample is shown in Figure 4-4. Keeping accurate records in your check register is very important. Doing so will help you identify any errors that you or the bank have made so that the errors can be corrected.

Your bank may offer electronic banking. **Electronic banking**, or online banking, is the transfer of funds by computer instead of using paper checks or cash. You can check your balance as often as needed online. If you do not use automated services, you can reconcile your account by using the form on the back of your bank statement. Just compare your bank statement with your checkbook to make sure the numbers are correct after adjustments.

Checks are paid within a few days, even if sent out of town, and may clear electronically as soon as the check is cashed. Once the check has been paid by your bank, it is a cancelled check and cannot be used again. If you pay your bills online, the payment amounts may clear almost immediately.

Never write a check for more money than you have in your account. If you write a check for more money than you have, this is called an **overdraft**. The bank may refuse to pay such a check. If the bank does pay the check, that

> **F.Y.I.** Overdrafts are also known as bounced checks.

Figure 4-3 Always keep your check register up to date.

Date	Ck #	Transaction	Debits		Credits		Balance
1/1		Initial deposit			1,125.00	✓	1,125.00
1/10		Check deposit			1,234.67	✓	2,359.67
1/12		Transfer to savings	150.00	✓			2,209.67
1/13	501	Void					2,209.67
1/13	502	Ace Realty, rent	410.00	✓			1,799.67
1/14	503	CTS for cable	29.95	✓			1,769.72
1/14	504	Access One, Internet service	35.40	✓			1,734.32
1/14	505	Dells Dept. Store for clothes	56.39	✓			1,677.93
1/14	506	Drugs, Inc. for medicine	12.54	✓			1,665.39
1/14	507	Elm Valley Electric for bill	55.84	✓			1,609.55
1/14	508	Municipal Utilities, water bill	29.18	✓			1,580.37
1/14	509	Reed's Garage, auto repair	165.32				1,415.05
1/14	510	Elm Valley Telephone, bill	54.28	✓			1,360.77
1/14	511	Sofa Hut, furniture	295.00	✓			1,065.77
1/14	512	Mobile Inc., cell phone bill	20.00	✓			1,045.77
1/14	513	Safe Storage, storage rental	43.29				1,002.48
1/15	514	EV College, tuition	145.00	✓			857.48
1/15	515	Food Basket for groceries	98.54	✓			758.94
1/18	ATM	Cash withdrawal	60.00	✓			698.94
1/19		Check deposit			84.10	✓	783.04
1/27	ATM	Cash withdrawal	60.00				723.04
1/28		Check deposit			75.00		798.04
1/28		Service fee	3.00				795.04

Payee — Checks and withdrawals — Checkmark indicates that item appears on bank statement — Deposits — Balance column

amount is basically considered a loan to you. You may have to pay hefty fees for this service. Your bank might charge $25 to $30 or more for an overdraft fee. If the bank does not pay the check, it is returned to the business or person to whom you gave it. You may have to pay $30 or more to the business for the returned check. Keep in mind that it is a criminal offense to deliberately write checks when you do not have enough funds in your account to pay for them.

Some banks offer **overdraft protection.** If you have this service, your check will be paid by the bank even if you do not have enough in your account to cover it. Customers have to sign up for this protection and pay a fee for this service. Read the terms carefully when considering signing up for overdraft protection. You should not need overdraft protection if you keep accurate records and always know how much money you have in your account.

Do not write a post-dated check. A **post-dated check** is a check with a date that is in the future. Suppose you ask someone to hold a post-dated check for a few days because you do not have enough money in your account for the check now. If the person cashes the check right away instead of holding it, the bank will charge you an overdraft fee. The bank might also refuse to cash the check because you do not have enough funds in the account.

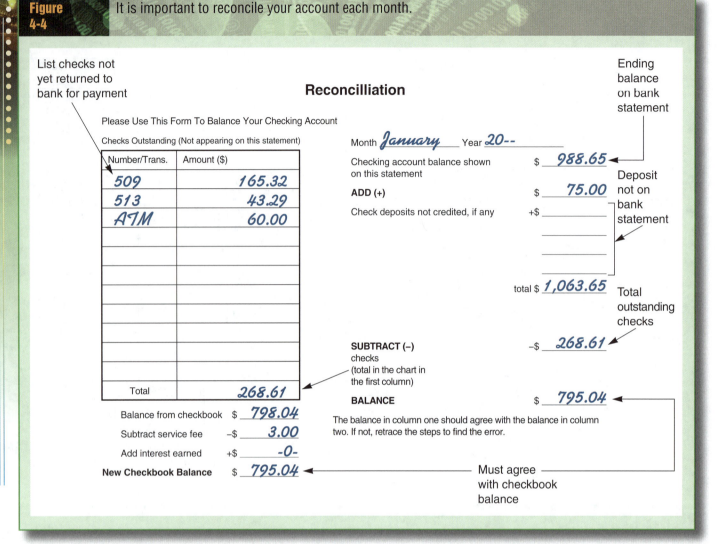

Figure 4-4 It is important to reconcile your account each month.

Example 4-2

You deposit $48 into a new checking account and later make another deposit of $10. You then write three checks for these amounts: $6.75, $13.20, and $17.32. Your bank charges a service charge of $5.50 per month. How much will you have left in your account at the end of the month?

Beginning balance		$48.00
Deposit		+ 10.00
Subtotal		$58.00
Check #1	$6.75	
Check #2	13.20	
Check #3	+ 17.32	
Total amount of checks		$37.27
Service charge		− 5.50
Ending balance		$15.23

You Do the Math 4-2

You deposit $138.47 in a new checking account. Later in the month, you make a deposit of $35 and write checks for $7.83, $14.98, $43.50, and $9.64. Your service charge is $8 per month. What is your balance at the end of the month?

Beginning balance	_____
Deposit	_____
Subtotal:	_____
Check #1	_____
Check #2	_____
Check #3	_____
Check #4	_____
Total amount of checks	_____
Service charge	_____
Ending balance	_____

Check Your Understanding

Why do you need to keep an accurate check register?

_____
_____

Check Register

1. Record the following entries in a check register, fill in the deposit slips, and write the checks. Use the current year in the dates. Use your signature on all checks. Use DC in the Ck # column for debit card purchases.

   April 1   Initial deposit of $175 cash into a checking account
   April 7   Check #163 to JeansWorld for new shirt for $37.78
   April 10   Check #164 to Pizzaland for pizza for $23.90
   April 12   Withdraw $20 cash from your ATM
   April 15   Deposit this week's paycheck for $58.60
   April 17   Check #165 to My Favorite CDs for birthday gifts for $19.45
   April 22   Withdraw $40 cash from your ATM
   April 25   Use debit card for purchase of $24.68 at Spring Shop for sandals
   April 27   Use debit card for ice cream at The Creamery for $6.78
   April 30   Bank statement shows a monthly service charge of $7.50

Date	Ck #	Transaction	Debits	Credits	Balance

2. Your bank statement for April shows a balance of $72.96. Checks 163 and 164, the two ATM withdrawals, and the two debit card purchases appear on the statement. The two deposits appear on the bank statement. Complete the reconciliation form to make sure your balance at the end of the month matches the bank statement balance.

Main St. Bank

DEPOSIT

Today's Date _____

Customer Name *(Please Print)*
_____

Sign Here *(If cash is received from this deposit)*
X _____

▼ Start your account number here
0 0 0 9 4 2 1 3 0 1 3 6 5 0   TOTAL $

CASH ▶
CHECK ▶
TOTAL FROM OTHER SIDE ▶
SUBTOTAL ▶
CASH BACK ▶

Student Name
1234 School Street
Anytown, USA 55615

_____
Date _____

Pay to
The Order of _____ $ _____

_____ dollars

Memo _____
Account # 0009-4213-:01-36-50

Chapter 4   Banking: Managing Your Money

Student Name
1234 School Street
Anytown, USA 55615   Date _____

Pay to
The Order of _____ $ _____

_____ dollars

Memo _____
Account # 0009-4213-:01-36-50

Main St. Bank

DEPOSIT

Today's Date _____

Customer Name *(Please Print)*
_____

Sign Here *(If cash is received from this deposit)*
X _____

▼ Start your account number here

| 0 | 0 | 0 | 9 | 4 | 2 | 1 | 3 | 0 | 1 | 3 | 6 | 5 | 0 | TOTAL $

CASH ▶
CHECK ▶
TOTAL FROM OTHER SIDE ▶
SUBTOTAL ▶
CASH BACK ▶

Student Name
1234 School Street
Anytown, USA 55615   Date _____

Pay to
The Order of _____ $ _____

_____ dollars

Memo _____
Account # 0009-4213-:01-36-50

Reconcilliation

Please Use This Form To Balance Your Checking Account

Checks Outstanding (Not appearing on this statement)

Number/Trans.	Amount ($)
Total	

Balance from checkbook $ _____

Subtract service fee   –$ _____

Add interest earned   +$ _____

New Checkbook Balance $ _____

Month _____ Year _____

Checking account balance shown $ _____
on this statement

ADD (+) $ _____

Check deposits not credited, if any   +$ _____

_____

_____

_____

total $ _____

SUBTRACT (–)   –$ _____
checks
(total in the chart in
the first column)

BALANCE $ _____

The balance in column one should agree with the balance in column two. If not, retrace the steps to find the error.

Savings Accounts

You may already have a savings account that was started for you when you were very young. When the account was opened, you received a savings account record that shows activity in the account. An example savings record is shown in Figure 4-5. Regular savings accounts provide a way to teach very young children how to save money and earn interest. These accounts do not pay very high rates of interest. However, savings accounts can be an important part of your financial plan because they are liquid. You can save money for a specific purpose or just to build a reserve for a rainy day. You may withdraw money at any time.

Chapter 4 Banking: Managing Your Money

Figure 4-5 If you have a savings account, your savings record may look similar to this one.

....SAVINGS ACCOUNT RECORD....

Learning Financial Institution
Anytown, USA 55615

Statement Savings Account

Account Number __00 - 1234__
Name __Student Name__
Address __1234 School Street__
        __Anytown, USA 55615__

Date	Credit/Deposits	Debit/Withdrawal	Account Balance	Memo
3/8	100 00		100 00	Initial Deposit
3/24	27 00		127 00	
4/3	32 00		159 00	
4/10		25 00	134 00	
4/30	68 00		202 00	
5/6	20 00		222 00	
5/14		12 50	209 50	
5/21	32 75		242 25	

Example 4-3

How much interest will you earn on a savings account in one year with a simple interest rate of 2% on a balance of $500?

Balance	$500.00
Interest rate	× .02
Total interest earned	$10.00

You Do the Math 4-3

How much interest will you earn in one year if your balance is $475 with an interest rate of 3%?

Balance	_____
Interest rate	_____
Total interest earned	_____

Remember compounding from Chapter 1? Interest on savings accounts is usually compounded on a daily, monthly, or quarterly basis. The more frequently the bank compounds, the more interest you will receive.

Example 4-4

How much more will your $500 savings account be worth in one year if your bank compounds interest quarterly?

Quarter	Beginning Balance	× .02 Interest Rate	× .25 Years	Ending Balance
1	$500.00	10.00	2.50	$502.50
2	502.50	10.05	2.51	505.01
3	505.01	10.10	2.53	507.54
4	507.54	10.15	2.54	510.08

Value of savings with compounded interest	$510.08
Value of savings with simple interest	− 510.00
Difference in earnings	$.08

The difference is insignificant in this example. However, with larger amounts and over a longer time period, the difference in earnings would increase. Remember the "magic of compounding" from Chapter 1? Having the interest compounded daily would also make a difference in the amount of interest earned.

You Do the Math 4-4

How much more will your savings account of $475 be worth in one year if your bank compounds interest quarterly?

Quarter	Beginning Balance	× .03 Interest Rate	× .25 Years	Ending Balance
1				
2				
3				
4				

Value of savings with compounded interest	_____
Value of savings with simple interest	_____
Difference in earnings	_____

Chapter 4 Banking: Managing Your Money

What is the advantage of having a savings account?

_____
_____
_____

Certificates of Deposit

Banks offer many other services along with checking and savings accounts. A **certificate of deposit** (CD) is an account that earns a higher rate of interest than a regular savings account. A set amount is deposited, usually a minimum of $500 to $1,000 or more. You agree to leave the amount on deposit for a certain length of time. For example, you may deposit $1,500 in a CD for one year. The bank guarantees a certain interest rate for that time period. If you withdraw the money early, you will not receive the full interest amount. You may also have to pay a penalty for early withdrawal. Although there are certain rules that banks must follow, the terms of CDs vary from bank to bank. See Figure 4-6 for an example of a CD.

> **F.Y.I.**
> The maturity date of a CD is the date when the money has been on deposit for the agreed upon amount of time. This is when you can collect the principal plus the interest earned.

Figure 4-6 Certificate of Deposit

Example 4-5

In an earlier example, $500 was deposited for one year at a rate of 2% in a savings account. If you deposit the same amount in a CD, you would earn more interest for the same period of time. However, you would not be able to withdraw your money until the maturity date (without paying a penalty). How much more interest would you earn if your $500 were in a CD earning 3%?

Deposit in savings	$500.00
Rate of interest	× .02
Interest earned	$10.00
Deposit in CD	$500.00
Rate of interest	× .03
Interest earned	$15.00
CD interest	$15.00
Savings interest	− 10.00
Difference	$5.00

You Do the Math 4-5

You deposit $1,000 into a savings account earning 0.75% interest. How much interest would you earn? How much more interest would you earn if you had put the same amount of money into a one-year CD earning 2.5% interest?

Deposit in savings	_____
Rate of interest	_____
Interest earned	_____
Deposit in CD	_____
Rate of interest	_____
Interest earned	_____
CD interest	_____
Savings interest	_____
Difference	_____

The actual yield is higher on a CD than the stated percentage rate because of compounding. This is called the **annual percentage yield** or **APY**. Most banks compound daily, which makes your money grow more quickly.

Chapter 4   Banking: Managing Your Money

CDs earn more than regular savings accounts because you commit to leaving your money in the bank for a certain time period. Although you may take the money out before the time period is up, you will be penalized with a withdrawal fee. You probably will not receive the full-term interest. You may receive interest for the amount of time you left the money on deposit. You might not get back your entire principal if the withdrawal penalty is high. Some banks set an early withdrawal fee, such as $25, plus a percent of the interest that would have been earned at full term. Again, different banks have different terms. Read the terms and conditions for the CD carefully so you can make informed decisions about your account.

Example 4-6

A $500 CD pays 3.5% interest. The term of the CD is one year. The penalty for withdrawing the money early is 50% of the full-term interest amount plus $25. How much interest will you earn on the CD if you leave it for the full term? How much will the penalty amount be if you withdraw all the money early?

Step 1   Calculate the amount of interest earned for the full term

Amount deposited	$500.00
Rate of interest	× .035
Interest earned	$17.50

Step 2   Multiply the interest earned for the full term times the penalty and add any set fee

Interest earned	$17.50
Penalty	× .5
Amount of penalty	$8.75
Early withdrawal fee	+ 25.00
Total penalty	$33.75

You Do the Math 4-6

You have a $1,200 CD that earns 3% interest. The term is one year. The penalty for withdrawing your money early is 75% of the full-term interest amount plus $20. How much interest will you earn on the CD if you leave it for the full term? How much will the penalty amount be if you withdraw all the money early?

Step 1   Calculate the amount of interest earned for full term

Amount deposited	_____
Rate of interest	_____
Interest earned	_____

Step 2 Multiply the interest earned for the full term times the penalty and add any set fee

Interest earned _____

Penalty _____

Amount of penalty _____

Early withdrawal fee _____

Total penalty _____

Check Your Understanding

Explain the difference between a regular savings account and a certificate of deposit. Why might you need to have both?

_____
_____
_____
_____
_____
_____
_____

Money Market Accounts

Money market accounts are checking accounts that pay interest on the amount you have deposited in the account. Money market accounts allow you to take money out any time you want. Generally, you are allowed to write a specific number of checks per month. However, for some accounts, it is required that a check be written for $100 or more. Money market accounts typically pay higher interest rates than checking accounts.

To get a high interest rate, you will probably have to keep a large minimum balance in your account. The amount might be $5,000 or more. If the balance falls below the required minimum, your interest rate may be reduced. As with checking accounts, you may have to pay a service charge for a money market account if your balance falls below a certain amount. In the following examples, annual interest is used. However, interest for money market accounts may be compounded more often, such as daily.

Example 4-7

How much interest would you earn for one year if you deposit $5,000 in a money market account earning 1.25% interest?

Deposit	$5,000.00
Interest rate	× .0125
Interest earned	$62.50

 Do the Math 4-7

You have $2,500 in a money market account earning 2.75% interest. How much interest will you earn in one year?

Deposit	_____
Interest rate	_____
Interest earned	_____

✓ Check Your Understanding

What are the advantages of a money market account?

_____

_____

Debit Cards

You may receive a debit card with your checking or savings account. A **debit card** is a plastic card that looks similar to a credit card. It allows users to pay for purchases by having the money drawn from a bank account. Debit cards provide a convenient way to pay for goods or services. They can be used in many retail stores and restaurants.

Debit cards are also called *bank cards* or *check cards*. They can also be used at an ATM. **ATM** stands for automated teller machine. ATMs allow users to perform various banking tasks. For example, you can use a debit card at an ATM to check your account balance or withdraw cash from your account. Typically, you must enter a password or ID number to complete the transaction. You may have to pay a fee to use the ATM.

Purchases

A debit card allows you to make purchases by swiping your card through a machine at the merchant's counter. The clerk may ask whether you want to use your card as a debit or credit. Before using as a debit card, ask whether the merchant charges a fee for the use of a debit card.

F.Y.I. Consider writing "SEE PHOTO ID" on the back of your debit card. The merchant then should ask for a photo ID before accepting the card. This should prevent someone else from using your card if it is lost or stolen.

Most banks offer debit cards as an alternative to using checks or cash to pay for goods or services.

Shutterstock

Every bank is different, so it is important to make sure you understand how a debit card works at your bank. Some cards issued by the bank can be used as a debit card or a credit card. Money is taken out of your account either way, but charges may be added if you use your card as a debit card.

When you purchase with a debit card, the money is taken out of your checking account immediately. This is different from using a credit card where the charges are not paid until you receive a statement at the end of the month. It is very easy to have an overdraft, so use a debit card wisely. Many overdrafts occur because of failure to record debit card purchases and withdrawals.

As with checking accounts, your bank may provide overdraft protection. This service may prevent embarrassment at having your purchase declined. However, like overdraft protection for checking accounts, you will pay a fee for having this safeguard. Once again, the best way to avoid these charges is to keep accurate records.

Example 4-8

Your retail store charges $1.50 every time you use your debit card for a purchase. How much will you pay if you use it four times in one month?

Charge per use	$1.50
Number of uses	× 4
Total charge to use card	$6.00

Chapter 4 Banking: Managing Your Money

You Do the Math 4-8

Your local retail store charges $1.25 each time you use your debit card. How much will you pay if you use it seven times in one month?

Charge per use	_____
Number of uses	_____
Total charge to use card	_____

ATM Withdrawals

You may use your debit card and an ATM to withdraw cash from your account. These machines may be outside your bank or in retail stores. ATMs allow you to get cash conveniently when your bank is closed. Your debit card may allow you to withdraw money from an ATM anywhere in the United States as well as in foreign countries.

However, be aware that you will probably pay a fee if you use an ATM from a bank other than your own. Those fees of $2 to $6 per withdrawal add up quickly. You could easily have $15 to $20 in fees each month in addition to your monthly service charges.

The balance shown on your ATM receipt is probably not correct if you have outstanding checks. An **outstanding check** is a check that has not yet been returned to the bank for payment. Be sure to factor in these checks when you calculate your balance—and always keep your register up to date.

F.Y.I. *You may be able to use your card as a credit card rather than a debit card. When doing so, you probably will not have to enter a PIN (personal identification number) for the transaction. This may be a safer choice because you do not have to worry that someone will steal your PIN by looking over your shoulder.*

Example 4-9

Your ATM receipt shows you have a balance of $142.38 in your checking account. You know you have written two checks for $6.39 and $8.17 that have not cleared the bank. What is your adjusted balance?

Balance on ATM receipt		$142.38
Check #1	$6.39	
Check #2	+ 8.17	
Total outstanding checks		− 14.56
Adjusted balance		$127.82

You Do the Math 4-9

The balance on your ATM receipt is $78.56. You just wrote a check this morning for $18.69. What is your adjusted balance?

Balance on ATM receipt	_____
Outstanding check	_____
Adjusted balance	_____

Check Your Understanding

What are two ways a debit card can be used?

_____

_____

FDIC Insurance

The **FDIC** (Federal Deposit Insurance Corporation) is an independent agency of the federal government. Its mission is to keep the financial system in the United States stable. It also seeks to promote public confidence in the system. The FDIC insures checking, savings, certificates of deposit, and money market accounts at most banks and most other financial institutions. This means that you will be able to withdraw your funds even if the bank closes. This is guaranteed by the federal government. Your bank should have a sign indicating it is a member of the FDIC.

Each account is currently insured up to $250,000 by the FDIC. However, this amount could change in future years. Make sure your checking, savings, and CD accounts are covered.

> **F.Y.I.**
> FDIC insurance began in January of 1934. The original amount of coverage was for deposits of $2,500.

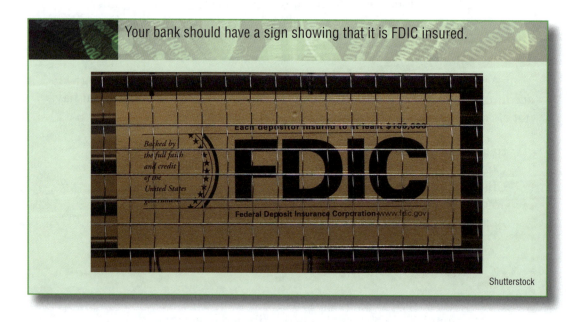

Your bank should have a sign showing that it is FDIC insured.

Shutterstock

Chapter 4   Banking: Managing Your Money

Check Your Understanding

What does FDIC stand for? Why is it important for your bank to be a member of this organization?

_____
_____
_____
_____

Bank Accounts

1. Visit the websites of at least three different banks in your area to research their services and fees. Check to see that each bank is insured by the FDIC. Complete the following chart with interest rates and fees for each type of account.

Bank Name	Checking Interest/Fees	Savings Interest/Fees	CDs Interest/Fees	Money Market Interest/Fees	Online Banking?	FDIC Ins.?

2. What accounts do these institutions offer high school or college students who may write fewer checks than older adults? Complete the following chart. If these institutions offer special checking accounts, write the special terms that students receive.

Bank Name	Checking for Students	Savings for Students	CDs for Students	Money Market for Students

3. Do these banks offer debits cards? If so, what are the fees? What are the fees if you overdraw your account?

Bank Name	Debit Card Yes/No	Debit Card Fees	Overdraft Fees

Other Financial Organizations

Two other types of organizations offer many of the same services that a bank offers. These organizations are savings and loan associations and credit unions. They are more specialized than regular banks. They may not offer the complete range of services that a full-service bank will have.

Savings and Loan Associations

A **savings and loan association**, sometimes called a thrift and loan, usually offers savings accounts, CDs, and checking account services. These associations earn money to pay interest on your accounts by issuing home mortgages. Savings and loan associations generally offer higher interest rates on savings than regular banks. Accounts in a savings and loan association are insured by the FDIC.

When would you use a savings and loan association?
_____
_____

Credit Unions

Another organization that offers financial services is a credit union. **Credit unions** are nonprofit cooperatives. They exist to serve their members. Members share something in common. For example, they may all be in the same profession, such as teachers. Typically, you must be a member to use the services of a credit union.

Credit unions usually pay interest on money you place on deposit. You may also be able to borrow money, often at a low interest rate. For example, you might borrow money for a car loan or home mortgage. Your deposits are insured in most credit unions by the National Credit Union Share Insurance Fund (NCUSIF).

Chapter 4   Banking: Managing Your Money   107

Who may use the services of a credit union?

_____

_____

Account Fees

1. Review the four common types of bank, credit union, or savings and loan association accounts: checking, savings, CDs, and money market accounts. For each, list the types of fees that each might charge.

Type of Account	Possible Fees
Checking	
Savings	
Certificates of Deposit	
Money Market	

2. What are the potential benefits of having each of these accounts?

Type of Account	Benefits
Checking	
Savings	
Certificates of Deposit	
Money Market	

Finding the Right Bank for You
A Checklist

When you are ready to open an account at the bank, do not just go to the bank that is most convenient. Shop around until you find the bank that is right for you. Much of your homework can be done online. Use this checklist to help you select the bank you will use.

Yes	No	
____	____	1. Do I know the type of identification I need to open an account?
____	____	2. Are student checking accounts or savings accounts available?
____	____	3. Do I know what interest is paid on the accounts?
____	____	4. Is there a monthly fee for an account?
____	____	5. Is there a charge for each check that I write?
____	____	6. Do I have to pay to have checks printed?
____	____	7. Will I have to keep a minimum balance in the account?
____	____	8. Does a debit card come with the account?
____	____	9. Is there a charge for using an ATM?
____	____	10. Can I check my balance, pay bills, and other services electronically?

Chapter Review

Summary

Banks are convenient, safe places to keep your money. You should make sure the bank you select is a member of the FDIC. Some services that banks offer are checking accounts, savings accounts, certificates of deposit, and money market accounts. For some accounts, banks pay interest but may also charge fees. Additional services, such as debit cards or electronic banking, come with some accounts. Debit cards provide a convenient way to pay for goods or services or to withdraw money using an ATM. Saving and loan associations and credit unions offer many of the same services that a bank offers. They are more specialized than banks and may not offer the complete range of services that a bank might offer.

Review Your Knowledge

Circle the correct answer for each of the following.

1. It is suggested that you keep how much money in a liquid account?
   A. One to two weeks' living expenses.
   B. One to two months' living expenses.
   C. Three to six months' living expenses.
   D. One year's living expenses.

2. A checking account may
   A. pay interest.
   B. require a minimum balance.
   C. have a service charge.
   D. All the above.

3. Of the accounts listed, which type usually pays the lowest interest rate?
   A. Checking account.
   B. Savings account.
   C. CD.
   D. Money market account.

4. You would probably not pay a fee in which of the following circumstances?
   A. Using an ATM for your own bank.
   B. Using an ATM for a different bank.
   C. Having an overdraft.
   D. Having under the minimum balance in a money market account.

5. For which type of account do you agree to leave your money on deposit for a certain period of time?
   A. Checking account.
   B. Savings account.
   C. Certificate of deposit.
   D. Money market account.

6. The FDIC currently insures bank accounts up to
   A. $100,000.
   B. $150,000.
   C. $200,000.
   D. $250,000.

7. A debit card purchase or withdrawal takes money out of your account
   A. immediately.
   B. in one or two days.
   C. in one week.
   D. in one month.

8. Checks that have been written but not returned to the bank for payment are called
   A. cancelled checks.
   B. overdrafts.
   C. outstanding checks.
   D. ATM withdrawals.

9. Who may deposit money into a credit union?
   A. Anyone.
   B. Members of the credit union.
   C. Only those who can deposit at least $5,000.
   D. Only those who want to borrow money from the credit union.

10. When completing a reconciliation for your bank account,
    A. you do not need to know which checks are outstanding.
    B. service fees charged by the bank are added to your check register balance.
    C. outstanding deposits are added to the bank statement balance.
    D. outstanding checks are added to the bank statement balance.

Build Your Vocabulary

For each word or term, write the correct definition using your own words.

11. Liquid

12. Service charge

13. Check register

14. Overdraft

15. Overdraft protection

16. Electronic banking

17. Postdated check

18. Annual percentage yield (APY)

19. Debit card

20. ATM

Apply Your Math Skills

Calculate the answers to the following problems.

21. Your bank charges $0.27 per check plus a service charge of $7.50. What fees would you pay for one month if you write six checks this month?

22. You make an initial deposit of $46.82 in a checking account. In addition, you deposit your paycheck of $78.36 at the end of the week. You write checks for $16.93, $26.25, $9.27, and $12.58. Your bank service charge is $6.95 per month. How much will you have in your account at the end of the month?

23. You make a deposit of $375 into a savings account and leave it for one year. How much interest will you earn in one year if the simple interest rate is 2.5%?

24. You deposit $1,500 in a savings account earning 3.5% simple interest. How much more interest would you earn if the bank compounds quarterly?

25. You can earn 3% interest on a CD and 1.25% interest on a savings account. How much more interest will the CD earn for one year if you make a deposit of $1,650?

26. You deposit $800 into a one-year CD that will earn 2.75% interest. The penalty for withdrawing the money early is 1.5 times the full-term interest plus $30. How much interest will you earn on the CD if you leave it for the full term? How much will the penalty amount be if you withdraw all the money early?

27. If you deposit $2,500 into a money market account earning 2.25% interest, how much interest will you earn in a year?

28. Your retail store charges $1.25 for each debit card purchase. How much will you pay for the month if you use your debit card to make two purchases from your retail store?

29. Your ATM receipt shows a balance of $149.81. You mailed checks this morning for $13.98 and $21.60. What is your adjusted balance?

30. Your ATM receipt shows a balance of $203.51 You mailed checks this morning for $130.78 and $75.00. What is your adjusted balance?

5 Credit: Buy Now, Pay Later

Terms

Credit history
Default
Cosigner
Capacity
Credit application
Capital
Credit bureau
Credit report
Credit score
Credit card
Unsecured loan
Collateral
Annual percentage rate (APR)
Revolving credit
Cash advance
Available credit
Bankruptcy
Chapter 7 bankruptcy
Chapter 13 bankruptcy

Objectives

When you complete Chapter 5, you will be able to:

- **Explain** the three Cs of credit.
- **Discuss** the importance of credit bureaus and what they do.
- **Explain** how credit cards work and list some of the considerations for using credit cards.
- **Discuss** two types of personal bankruptcy.

Chapter 5   Credit: Buy Now, Pay Later

Before you read this chapter, answer the following questions to see how much you already know about credit.

1. Can anyone get a credit card?

2. A credit application cannot ask you for your age, race, sex, nationality, or religion. Why do you think this is the law?

3. What are some causes of credit problems? How can credit problems be avoided?

4. How can you be a smart credit card user?

5. Do you know what is on a credit report?

6. Do you know where to get a credit report?

7. What is a FICO score?

8. How do needs and wants become important when using a credit card?

9. What is credit history and why is it important?

10. Do you know what the liability is for unauthorized use of a credit card?

Credit

Are you obsessed with *stuff*? Do you always want the newest clothes, video games, or cell phones? Do you know someone who rents a storage space to keep all the extra stuff she or he will probably never use? How do people buy all this stuff? Many people are disciplined enough to only buy what they need or can afford. Others, though, do not seem to worry if they lack the cash for what they want. They just pull out the "plastic" and charge it without thinking about how they will pay for it.

Using credit will be an important part of your financial planning. It will be important for you to learn to use credit wisely and make the right decisions as to when to charge purchases and when to pay cash. Credit is not cheap, and it will tie up your future income. So use it wisely.

How do you earn the privilege of using credit? Is it easy to obtain? In the late 2000s, credit was readily available to most people. All a person had to do was "sign on the dotted line" and money was easily accessible. Credit was cheap and easy to get. As a result, however, many people got into financial trouble. They lost many of their assets because they could not pay off their debts.

Getting credit has changed quite a bit since the early 2000s. Lenders look at the borrower's character, capacity, and capital before credit is extended. These things are called the "three Cs of credit."

Character

Lenders look at your character to judge your willingness to pay off debt. How do lenders determine whether you have the desire to pay back what you borrow? They look at your **credit history**, or the record of your prior credit purchases and payments. Have you paid your bills on time or are you consistently late with payments? To **default** means that you fail to pay a debt or other obligation. Have you ever defaulted on a loan or other debt? Businesses look for honesty and stability in those who are applying for credit. They want to know how long you have been at the same job or how often you have moved.

If you have never had credit, it may be difficult to get a loan. You might want a loan for your first car, for example. You may need someone, such as a parent or guardian, to cosign the loan for you because you lack a credit history. A **cosigner** is someone who agrees to pay your debt if you fail to pay. Keep in mind that the cosigner must have a good credit record or your loan may be denied.

Capacity

Capacity, as it relates to credit, is your ability to pay debts. Do you have a job? If so, do you earn enough to make the payments you agree to make? Do you change jobs frequently? What level of education do you have? All these are questions that would be asked on a **credit application**, a form that you will fill out in order to be considered for a loan.

In addition to information about your job, a lender will also want to know about other debts you have. The lender will ask you to list all your financial obligations, both the total amounts that you owe as well as the monthly payments for each debt. Even with a large income, too much debt may prevent you from being approved for additional credit.

F.Y.I.

If you are a high school student applying for credit or a job, you may be asked how many days of school you miss each year. Lenders may consider it a sign of instability if you have many absences without a good reason for them, such as illness.

Chapter 5 Credit: Buy Now, Pay Later 117

Credit Card Application

Complete the following application for a credit card.

CREDIT APPLICATION	EMPLOYEE NO.	DATE
	Type of Account Requested: ☐ INDIVIDUAL ☐ JOINT	

PLEASE TELL US ABOUT YOURSELF

FIRST NAME (TITLES OPTIONAL)	MIDDLE INITIAL	LAST NAME		AGE
STREET ADDRESS (IF P.O. BOX — PLEASE GIVE STREET ADDRESS)		CITY	STATE	ZIP

| ☐ OWN ☐ LIVE WITH RELATIVE | MONTHLY PAYMENT | YEARS AT PRESENT ADDRESS | HOME PHONE NO. | NO. OF |
| ☐ RENT ☐ OTHER | $ | | ( ) | DEPENDENTS |

PREVIOUS ADDRESS	CITY	STATE	ZIP	HOW LONG

NAME OF NEAREST RELATIVE NOT LIVING WITH YOU	RELATIONSHIP	PHONE NO. ( )
ADDRESS	CITY	STATE

NOW TELL US ABOUT YOUR JOB

EMPLOYER OR INCOME SOURCE	POSITION/TITLE	HOW LONG EMPLOYED YRS. MOS.	MONTHLY INCOME $
EMPLOYER'S ADDRESS	CITY	STATE	TYPE OF BUSINESS	BUSINESS PHONE ( )

MILITARY RANK (IF NOW IN SERVICE)	SEPARATION DATE	UNIT AND DUTY STATION

SOURCE OF OTHER INCOME (Alimony, child support, or separate maintenance need not be revealed if you do not wish to have it considered as a basis for repaying this obligation)	SOURCE	INCOME $	☐ MONTHLY ☐ ANNUALLY

AND YOUR CREDIT REFERENCES ARE

NAME AND ADDRESS OF BANK/SAVINGS AND LOAN	☐ CHECKING ☐ SAVINGS ☐ LOAN	PREVIOUS ACCOUNT? ACCOUNT NO. HOW IS ACCOUNT LISTED?	☐ YES ☐ NO

List Bank cards, Dept. Stores, Finance Co.'s, and other accounts:	NAME	ACCOUNT NO.	BALANCE	PAYMENT
			$	$
			$	$
			$	$
			$	$

INFORMATION REGARDING JOINT APPLICANT

COMPLETE THIS AREA IF ☐ JOINT ACCOUNT IS REQUESTED ☐ YOU ARE RELYING ON SPOUSE'S INCOME OR CREDIT HISTORY TO OBTAIN CREDIT

FIRST NAME	MIDDLE INITIAL	LAST NAME	AGE	RELATIONSHIP

JOINT APPLICANT'S ADDRESS IF DIFFERENT FROM APPLICANT			
ADDRESS	CITY	STATE	ZIP

JOINT APPLICANT'S PRESENT EMPLOYER	ADDRESS	HOW LONG EMPLOYED YRS. MOS.

BUSINESS PHONE ( )	POSITION/TITLE	MONTHLY INCOME $

YOUR SIGNATURE PLEASE

Store Stamp Below

I have read and agree to the Terms and Conditions of the Charge Agreement as set forth on attached. The credit card company is authorized to investigate my credit record and exchange credit experience with other creditors and Credit Reporting Agencies. This information is given to obtain credit, and is true and complete.

FOR OFFICE USE ONLY
Letter _____
CB. RPT. _____
EMP. VER _____

Applicant's Signature _____ Date

Joint Applicant's signature
(required if joint applicant section completed) _____ Date

DATE	EMP.	#CARDS	T/C	CR/LN.	APPROVED
☐	☐	☐	☐	☐	☐

Capital

Capital is the assets you have at your disposal. How much cash do you have in a savings account? Do own a house? Do you own a car? In Chapter 1, you learned about net worth. Many lenders will ask you to list your assets and liabilities to determine your net worth. Are your assets enough to cover the liabilities that you already have? If you lost your job, would you be able to use money from your savings to pay debts? Having money to pay your creditors is another reason why it is important to have that three to six months' cash reserve as mentioned in Chapter 4.

How do capital and capacity differ as they relate to credit?

_____
_____

Three Cs of Credit

Make a list of three questions a lender might ask about each of the three Cs of credit to determine whether you would qualify for a loan.

Character
   1. _____
   2. _____
   3. _____

Capacity
   1. _____
   2. _____
   3. _____

Capital
   1. _____
   2. _____
   3. _____

Credit Bureaus

How will a prospective lender find out about your credit history to decide whether to lend you money? From the time you get your first loan or credit card, the amounts you borrow and your payments will be faithfully tracked by a credit bureau. A **credit bureau** is an organization that keeps track of credit that is extended to you and the payments you make. The information is sold to others for a fee. Three major credit bureaus are Equifax, Experian, and TransUnion.

Businesses request information from these credit bureaus about potential customers and their histories for paying their bills. Payments, as well as late payments, are reported monthly to these credit bureaus. This helps keep your credit history up to date.

Credit Reports

Equifax, Experian, and TransUnion keep track of your credit history. These bureaus will issue a **credit report**. The report shows credit cards, car loans, mortgages, or any other type of credit that has been extended to you. It also shows payments you make and current balances on your accounts. Your credit report shows accounts that you have opened or closed and any current balances. Any claims from collection agencies, late payments, or defaults are included. The report may list employment information and current and former addresses. Lenders use the reports when deciding whether they will extend credit to you.

You can receive a free copy of your credit report every 12 months from each of the three bureaus by going to www.annualcreditreport.com and completing the required information. You can also order by phone or request an application by mail. Even if you have excellent credit, it is a good idea to get a copy of your report at least every couple of years. This lets you be sure your credit report is accurate. You should report any errors on your report immediately.

A credit report is one of the most important reports you will use in your adult life. It may help determine whether you can get a loan for a car or a house or rent an apartment. You should use credit wisely and check your credit report often to be sure it is correct.

FICO Credit Score

Your **credit score** is a number that indicates how well you handle credit. It is also called a FICO score, named for the Fair Isaac Corporation, a company that developed the rating system. Equifax, Experian, and TransUnion keep track of your FICO scores as well as your credit reports. The FICO score assembles all the information in your credit report and calculates a single number to indicate your credit worthiness. Negative reports may stay on your credit report for seven to ten years.

Lenders will check your credit score when you apply for credit, so it is very important to keep this number high. The range of numbers used for credit scores by credit bureaus, lenders, and government agencies varies a bit. Typical scores and ratings from 500 to 850 are shown in Figure 5-1. Although ratings from different sources vary, a score above 720 is considered excellent. A good score is 700 or more. You may be given limited or no credit if your score is below 500. The higher your score, the lower the interest rate you may be able to get on a loan.

> **F.Y.I.**
> Although credit reports may be obtained annually at no cost, you will usually have to pay for a FICO score. If you apply for a loan, however, your lender should be able to inform you of your FICO score.

Credit Report Application

Complete the following application that is used to request a credit report.

Credit Report Application

PLEASE PROVIDE ALL OF THE PERSONAL INFORMATION REQUIRED BELOW.

This information is needed to begin the process of determining your identity and finding your credit report. Please refer to our Privacy Policy to learn more about the use of and protection of this information.

First Name	Middle Initial	Last Name	Suffix

Date of Birth

Month	Day	Year (YYYY)

Current Address

Line 1

Line 2

City	State	Zip Code

Have you lived at your current address for at least two years?

Yes	No (If 'No,' please provide previous address)

Previous Address

Line 1

Line 2

City	State	Zip Code

FICO Scores

1. Search the web for information on credit reports and FICO scores to see what factors determine your credit score. List three things that increase your score.

   _____

   _____

2. List three things that decrease your score.

   _____

   _____

Figure 5-1 FICO Credit Score Chart

FICO Score	Rating
720–850	Excellent (This score range qualifies you for the best financing and interest rates.)
700–719	Very Good (This range qualifies you for favorable financing and interest rates.)
675–699	Average (This score range usually qualifies you for most loans.)
620–674	Sub Prime (You may qualify for a loan, but pay a higher interest rate.)
560–619	Risky (You will have trouble getting a loan.)
500–559	Very Risky (You need to improve your score before applying for a loan.)

To keep your FICO score high, pay your bills on time. Approximately 35% of your score is based on payment history. Keep your debt low and do not become overextended by buying more than you can afford. If your score is low, paying bills on time and keeping your balances low will significantly improve your score—sometimes within a few months. Be responsible with credit and check your FICO score often.

Example 5-1

If you have a FICO score of 765, you can borrow money at 4.5% interest. If your score is 500, you will have to pay 7% interest. How much less will you pay in simple interest in one year on a loan of $6,500 if you have the higher score?

Step 1 Calculate interest at 4.5%

Loan balance	$6,500.00
Interest rate	× .045
Annual interest at 4.5%	$292.50

Step 2 Calculate interest at 7%

Loan balance	$6,500.00
Interest rate	× .07
Annual interest at 7%	$455.00

Step 3 Calculate the difference

Interest at 7%	$455.00
Interest at 4.5%	− 292.50
Difference	$162.50

You Do the Math 5-1

Your FICO score is an excellent 780, and you can borrow $8,000 at 3.25%. Your friend's score is 525, and she will have to pay 7.5% for the same amount. How much less will you pay in simple interest in one year with the higher score than your friend will pay?

Step 1 Calculate interest at 3.25%

Loan balance _____

Interest rate _____

Annual interest at 3.25% _____

Step 2 Calculate interest at 7.5%

Loan balance _____

Interest rate _____

Annual interest at 7.5% _____

Step 3 Calculate the difference

Interest at 7.5% _____

Interest at 3.25% _____

Difference _____

Check Your Understanding

What are the names of the three major credit bureaus discussed in this chapter? Why should you check your credit report frequently?

_____

_____

_____

Credit Cards

Is what you want today worth spending your future income? Using credit can be very tempting, and young people are prime targets for companies that issue credit cards. However, credit plays a very important part in your financial planning. A **credit card** is a thin plastic card that contains information, such as a person's name and account number. It allows the holder (person whose card it is) to make purchases and pay for them at a later time. There are advantages of using credit cards. Credit cards enable you to shop online, carry less cash in your wallet, and pay for items needed when there are emergencies. However, you should resist the temptation to overspend. Remember, you have to pay this money back.

Most credit card purchases are considered an unsecured loan. An **unsecured loan** means that you can borrow money or purchase goods or services by just signing your name. Your signature confirms an agreement to pay the debt. You do not have to provide **collateral**, which is property accepted as security for a debt. You do, however, have an obligation to pay these unsecured debts, and you are legally accountable for them.

In some instances, you must pay interest for the privilege of using a credit card. For some cards, you may also have to pay a set annual fee. The interest rate that you will be charged is known as the **annual percentage rate (APR)**. When you start looking for a credit card, shop around to see which lender offers the lowest APR and has the lowest (or no) annual fee. Some lenders offer special credit cards with lower APRs for teens.

Your credit card will have a limit on how much you can purchase. Based on your credit history and ability to pay, the lender will set a limit on how much you can charge. Going over this limit could cost you a hefty fee, so be aware of the limit the bank has set.

Always guard your personal information when applying for a credit card. Make sure you know who the lender is when you give your Social Security number or other information. Once you get your card, do not let others borrow it. Make sure you know where your card is at all times.

F.Y.I.

In the 1950s, Diners Club was the first card that could be used at multiple locations. Before then, credit cards were issued for use only at a particular company, such as a store or gas station.

Being Financially Responsible

Handling a Credit Card
A Checklist

Having credit is a privilege and should be taken seriously. Good credit is an asset that will help you in the future. Bad credit is a liability that may keep you from having the things that you need or want. How would you rate your "credit personality"?

Yes   No

1. I always want more of everything and am not satisfied with what I have.
2. I tend to buy things because my friends have them, even when I really cannot afford them.
3. I am strong enough to resist impulse buying.
4. I am willing to give up the income I will have in the future to buy things I want but may not be able to afford now.
5. I know that I should pay my credit card statement in full each month.
6. I think that I really need a credit card. I do not want one just because all my friends have one.
7. I understand what credit history means and its importance to my future.
8. I know what a FICO score is and its importance.
9. I understand that I should only have one credit card at first.
10. I will not charge anything that I know I cannot afford.

Purchases

Almost all businesses accept some form of credit card—even fast-food restaurants. Most businesses accept major bank credit cards such as Visa, MasterCard, and American Express. However, some businesses, such as Sears, Kohls, and Target, also offer their own credit cards. Store charge cards usually offer special discounts and other offers to get customers to use their cards instead of bankcards.

Credit terms and agreements vary for credit cards. Some cards require you to pay the entire balance each month and do not charge interest. However, there may be a set annual fee for the card. Other cards do not require that you pay the full amount each month. You must pay only part of the charges, but you will be charged interest on the remaining amount. This type of account is known as **revolving credit**.

Chapter 5 Credit: Buy Now, Pay Later

Many cards with revolving credit have a grace period, a time during which you can pay your bill before any finances charges begin. The grace period is typically 20 to 25 days. Not all cards have a grace period, so read the credit agreement carefully. If you do not pay all charges in full each month, you must make a minimum payment. The minimum payment required by the bank or store issuing your credit card is the least amount you are required to pay that month.

Example 5-2

You have a zero balance (no charges) on your credit card. Then you charge $260 for back-to-school clothes. If your minimum payment is 5% of the balance, what will be your minimum payment?

Statement balance	$260.00
Minimum payment percentage	× .05
Minimum payment	$13.00

You Do the Math 5-2

You have a zero balance on your credit card. Then you charge a total of $600 on your credit card this month. Your minimum payment is 3% of the balance. What will be your minimum payment?

Statement balance	_____
Minimum payment percentage	_____
Minimum payment	_____

With a revolving credit card account, you could be charged interest on the amounts not paid during the grace period. The interest rate could be 20% or more. Before you decide to buy, consider whether you can pay the charge bill for that item at the end of the month. If not, you should calculate the cost of the credit as an additional cost of the item. That "bargain" is not a good deal if you pay minimum payments and interest for the next several months or years.

Financial calculators are available on the Internet. These programs let you see about how long it will take to pay off balances at various interest rates. A sample calculator is shown in Figure 5-2. The methods used by banks to calculate credit card balances on which you pay interest charges vary. Therefore, the results shown for the online calculators may not match those for your account exactly. However, the results will give you an idea of the payments needed. For example, suppose you have a charge of $260. The APR is 18%. If you make a minimum payment of $15 per month, it would take 21 months to pay off the charge and the related interest. To avoid paying interest, charge only what you can pay for in full when you receive your monthly statement.

Check Your Understanding

If you have a credit card that is a revolving account, why would you want the card to have a grace period for purchases?

_____

_____

Figure 5-2 Financial Calculator

Credit Card Payment Calculator

Credit balance	$260.00
APR	18%
Monthly payment amount	$15.00
Display results (monthly or yearly)	monthly

Calculate

Results

Number of monthly payments required to pay off the balance:	21
Interest amount:	$43.00

Financial Calculator

1. Find a financial calculator online. Use a search term such as *credit card payment calculator*.

2. Using the calculator, fill in the following chart to see how many months it will take to pay off these credit card balances.

Balance	Interest Rate	Monthly Payment	Months to Pay Off
$5,000	18%	$150	
350	16%	25	
12,000	12%	200	
1,650	10%	100	
3,600	8%	50	

Credit cards allow you to purchase things now and pay for them later.

Cash Advances

You may obtain a cash advance with your credit card when you need cash to make a purchase (rather than making a credit purchase). A **cash advance** is a loan against the available credit on your card. **Available credit** is the difference between your card's credit limit and the amount of credit you have already used.

Many times, the bank will mail you blank checks to use. These checks allow you to make purchases or to deposit money into your checking account to use any way you wish. Use these checks wisely because they are treated as a cash advance. You begin paying interest on the amount immediately. Even if you pay the amount by the due date, you will be charged interest. You can also obtain a cash advance at the bank that issued your card or by phone or online. There is usually a transaction fee of 2% to 5% of the amount you borrow, and the interest rate may be higher than on charge amounts for the purchases you make.

Example 5-3

You receive blank checks for cash advances from your bank. Your credit card limit is $6,000. You have already made purchases of $900 using the credit card. The transaction fee is 3% of the advance. What is your available credit? How much will you owe as a transaction fee if you write a cash advance check for that amount?

Step 1 Calculate your available credit

Credit limit	$6,000.00
Credit used	− 900.00
Available credit	$5,100.00

Step 2 Calculate the transaction fee

Cash advance	$5,100.00
Transaction fee percentage	× .03
Transaction fee	$153.00

It will cost you $153 just to borrow the money. In addition, you will pay interest for the loan. If you must pay 18% or 20% interest, this will be a very expensive way to borrow money.

You Do the Math 5-3

You want a cash advance on your credit card. Your credit card limit is $4,500. You have charged $1,200 on the card. The transaction fee is 2% of the cash advance. What is your available credit? How much will you owe as a transaction fee if you write a cash advance check for that amount?

Step 1 Calculate your available credit

Credit limit	_____
Credit used	_____
Available credit	_____

Step 2 Calculate the transaction fee

Cash advance	_____
Transaction fee percentage	_____
Transaction fee	_____

Check Your Understanding

Explain how a credit card can be used for cash advances.

_____

_____

Credit Card Fees

There are laws that regulate lenders and provide some protection to credit card holders. However, there are several fees related to credit cards that banks can charge. Some of those charges are described below.

- You may be charged penalties for late payments (even one day late).
- You can be charged a fee for going over your credit limit.
- You can be charged an annual fee for having a credit card if that is part of the credit agreement.
- You may be charged a fee for a check written in payment for your credit card balance if it does not clear your bank. Make sure you have enough money in your checking account to cover the check you write to the credit card company.
- Banks can increase your interest rate if they can justify doing so. Required minimum payments also may be increased.

F.Y.I. If you pay your credit card bills on time, banks will sometimes automatically raise your available credit limit. If you do not want them to do this, you can call the bank and request that your limit stay the same.

Example 5-4

Your bank charges a $20 fee for going over your limit and $25 for a late payment. If you do both in the same month, how much will you pay for these fees?

Over limit fee	$20.00
Late payment fee	+ $25.00
Total fees	$45.00

You Do the Math 5-4

Your bank fees are $28 for going over your limit and $27.50 for late payments. If you do both in the same month, how much will you pay for these fees?

Over limit fee	_____
Late payment fee	_____
Total fees	_____

Be selective when choosing a credit card! Although you may not be able to get the best rates for your first card, your goal should be to have a card with no annual fee and the lowest interest rate possible. Of course, if you always pay in full each month, the interest rate will not be quite so important! Make sure you only buy what you can afford to pay for in full at the end of each month to avoid paying interest or service charges. Avoid "prestige" cards that charge annual fees of $50 to $500 just to carry their card.

> **F.Y.I.**
> Beware of "teaser rates" that are only good on your credit card for a few months. Another low rate might only be available if you are transferring balances from other cards. These rates may be as high as 15% to 18% after those initial months of low rates.

Check Your Understanding

What kinds of penalty fees might your bank charge on your credit card?
_____
_____

Credit Card Statements

It is not uncommon for students to have $5,000 or more in credit card debt by the time they leave college. What do college students use credit cards for? Is it books and tuition or pizza, entertainment, and clothes? Do you really want to pay for that pizza for the next five years? Many college students do exactly that if they leave college with credit card debt.

Look carefully at Figure 5-3. Credit card statements must show how long it will take you to pay off your balance if you make only the minimum payment. Notice that with a balance of only $152.33 and an interest rate of 24.5% it would take five years to pay off your balance. You would pay $275 in interest! Also, notice the change in the minimum payment and the additional fees that may be charged. Your monthly statement would also list the purchases you have made. Always check to see if the charges on your card are for purchases you have made.

Truth in Lending

Do a search on a bank website for the Truth in Lending Disclosure statement. Print this statement and read the fine print. Write several paragraphs about what this statement means to you as a consumer.

_____
_____
_____
_____
_____
_____
_____

Figure 5-3: Credit Card Statement Example

Account Statement

For the period ending Aug 9, 20-- Days in billing cycle: 31
Questions or lost/stolen card? Call Customer Service 1-800-555-1234
Account Number: XXXX-XXXX-XXXX-XXXX
Page: 1 of 4

Summary of Account Activity

Previous Balance	$0.00
Payments	$0.00
Other Credits/Adjustments	$0.00
Purchases	+$152.33
Cash Advances	$0.00
Fees Charged	$0.00
Interest Charged	$0.00
Total New Balance	**$152.33**
Past Due Amount	$0.00
Credit Limit	$3000.00
Credit Available	$2847.00

Payment Information

Total New Balance	$152.33
Minimum Payment Due	$5.00
Payment Due Date	Sep 9, 20--

Late Payment Warning: If we do not receive your minimum payment by the date listed above, you may have to pay a Late Payment Fee of up to $25.00.

Minimum Payment Warning: If you make only the minimum payment each period, you will pay more in interest and it will take you longer to pay off your balance. For example:

If you make no additional charges using this card and each month you pay…	You will pay off the balance shown on this Statement in about…	And you will end up paying an estimated total of…
Only the minimum payment	5 years	$275
$6	3 years	$217 (Savings=$58)

If you are experiencing financial difficulty and would like information about credit counseling or debt management services, you may call 1-800-123-4567.

Bankruptcy

Bankruptcy is a legal decision that a person, company, or organization is unable to pay debts owed. More than one million Americans file for personal bankruptcy each year. A large number of them are young adults under the age of 25. Bankruptcy provides a way for people to cope with large debts that they cannot find a way to pay. Some people have large debts because they have managed their money poorly or spent unwisely. However, other people have large debts from situations not in their control. For example, many people file for bankruptcy because of overwhelming medical bills.

Bankruptcy laws are divided into chapters, with two main types of personal bankruptcies. A **chapter 7 bankruptcy**, also called straight bankruptcy, eliminates most types of debt. It stays on your credit report for 10 years. You must turn over your property to be sold to pay your creditors (people to whom you owe money). You may be allowed to keep your home, car, and other personal items (called exemptions) if you file for chapter 7 bankruptcy. The laws regarding property that can be exempt vary by state.

A **chapter 13 bankruptcy** provides a payment plan, allowing payments to a trustee who will pay your creditors for you. Payments should be lower than what you currently have been making. A chapter 13 plan represents at least an effort to repay your creditors. You usually get to keep the assets you own while lowering some of your interest and penalties. A chapter 13 bankruptcy stays on your credit report for seven years.

FYI: Filing bankruptcy does not eliminate student loans or unpaid taxes. You will still be responsible for paying these debts.

Bankruptcy should be used only as a last resort. Any type of bankruptcy lowers your credit score and stays on your credit record for years. This can make it very difficult to get credit.

There are laws that protect the consumer from lender abuse. If you have any questions about credit, seek advice from a professional to learn about your rights as a consumer.

Check Your Understanding

What is the difference between chapter 7 and chapter 13 bankruptcies?

___

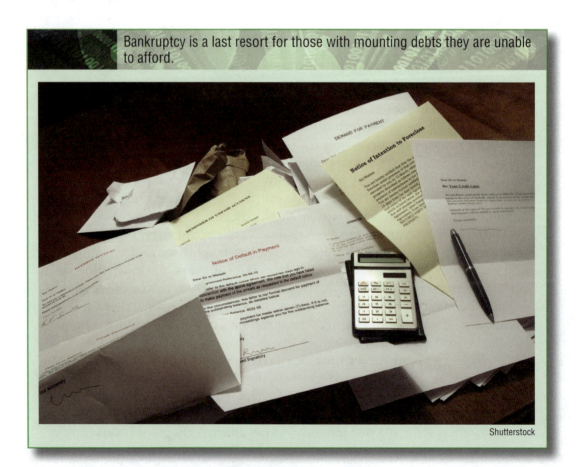

Bankruptcy is a last resort for those with mounting debts they are unable to afford.

Shutterstock

Dollars and $ense

Are you ready for a credit card?

"Your credit card can be used anywhere a Debit MasterCard is accepted."

How many times have you seen this line? The advertisement forgets to tell you that you still have to pay for whatever you purchase. You might not pay today. However, when you get your credit card bill, you will have to pay for the purchases. Do you think you will have more money in 30 days when the bill arrives than you have today? If you do not have the money to pay the bill in full, you could be charged some hefty interest payments.

Credit cards are a big responsibility that should not be taken lightly. It is very tempting to use a credit card for your immediate needs or wants. But remember, you still have to pay for the purchases.

If you think you are responsible enough to have your own credit card, do some homework before you apply for one. Answer the following questions as you think about getting a credit card.

- ❑ Will I need a cosigner when I open an account?
- ❑ Are there any fees associated with opening an account? If so, how much are they?
- ❑ Am I required to pay the balance in full each month?
- ❑ Are there late fees if I miss the date to pay the bill?
- ❑ What is the interest rate?
- ❑ How is the finance charge calculated on unpaid balances?
- ❑ Is there a monthly fee or annual fee that is charged for having the credit card?
- ❑ Is there a credit limit, and will it be raised automatically if I pay on time?
- ❑ Can I use the card as a debit card and credit card?
- ❑ Does the bank offer any fraud insurance for the card?

If you decide you are responsible enough to manage a credit card, remember to use it wisely. At first, get only one credit card that you can use in most stores where you generally shop. Keep the credit card in a safe place to protect your identity. Do not let your friends borrow your credit card. Be responsible, respect the limits, and pay the balance every month.

If your credit card is lost or stolen, you are only liable for $50 no matter how much has been charged on it. However, there are steps you should take immediately if that happens. Keep a record of all your credit card numbers in a safe place. Call the credit card company immediately to report a lost or stolen card. Also, contact the three major credit bureaus to let them know your card has been lost or stolen to prevent damage to your credit report.

Chapter Review

Summary

Using credit will be an important part of your financial planning. You should learn to use credit wisely and make the right decisions as to when to charge purchases and when to pay cash. Lenders look at the "three Cs of credit" (character, capacity, and capital) for a borrower before credit is extended. Lenders get information about your credit history in the form of a credit report from credit bureaus. Your credit score, a number that indicates how well you handle credit, is also considered when you apply for credit. Many people use credit cards to make purchases or get cash advances. If you do not pay the full balance for the card each month, you may be charged interest. Finance charges (interest and other fees) for credit cards can be quite high. You should check your credit card statements carefully and be informed about interest and fees that may apply to your account. People who cannot pay their debts may file for bankruptcy. Bankruptcy is a legal decision stating that a person is unable to pay debts owed. Bankruptcy should always be a last resort. Any type of bankruptcy lowers your credit score and stays on your credit record for years.

Review Your Knowledge

Circle the correct answer for each of the following.

1. Which of the following relates to your willingness to pay back debt?
   A. character
   B. capacity
   C. capital
   D. credit report

2. A record of all your credit purchases and payments is called a(n)
   A. credit bureau.
   B. capital amount.
   C. credit history.
   D. available credit amount.

3. Someone who signs for you to be able to get credit is a
   A. character.
   B. credit bureau.
   C. lender.
   D. cosigner.

4. Which of the following has to do with your ability to pay off debt?
   A. character
   B. capacity
   C. available credit
   D. credit report

5. An agency that keeps track of your credit history and FICO scores is a(n)
   A. cosigner.
   B. credit bureau.
   C. lender.
   D. employer.

6. You can obtain a copy, without cost, of which of these each year?
   A. Credit payments.
   B. Credit report.
   C. Credit score.
   D. Credit application.

7. A FICO score is also known as a
   A. credit report.
   B. credit history.
   C. credit card.
   D. credit score.

8. The amount of credit you have left to use to reach your credit card limit is your
   A. minimum payment.
   B. available credit.
   C. interest rate.
   D. cash advance.

9. The amount you must pay on your credit card each month is called a(n)
   A. minimum payment.
   B. available credit amount.
   C. interest rate.
   D. cash advance.

10. Which of the following provides a payment plan to pay off debt?
    A. Cash advance.
    B. Chapter 7 bankruptcy.
    C. Chapter 13 bankruptcy.
    D. Cosigner.

Build Your Vocabulary

For each word or term, write the correct definition using your own words.

11. Default

_____

_____

12. Cosigner

13. Credit application

14. Capital

15. Credit report

16. Credit card

17. Unsecured loan

18. Collateral

19. Minimum payment

20. Chapter 7 bankruptcy

21. Chapter 13 bankruptcy

Apply Your Math Skills

Calculate the answers to the following problems.

22. Your FICO score of 790 enables you to obtain a loan for $6,500 at 3.5% interest. Your friend needs the same amount. However, because his FICO score is 600, he will have to pay 6% interest. How much less will you pay in simple interest in one year for the same amount of money?

    _____

    _____

23. You have a zero balance (no charges) on your credit card. Then you buy a new cell phone and music downloads with your credit card this month for a total of $265. Your minimum payment is 6% of the balance. What will be your minimum payment?

    _____

    _____

24. You want a cash advance on your credit card. The transaction fee is 3% of the cash advance. Your credit card limit is $3,800. You have purchases of $850.00 on the card. What is your available credit? How much will you owe as a transaction fee if you write a cash advance check for that amount?

    _____

    _____

25. Your bank charges $23 for a late payment and a fee of $28.50 for going over your limit. If you do both in the same month, how much will you pay for these fees?

    _____

    _____

6 Insurance: Protecting Your Assets

Terms

- Risk
- Insurance
- Collision coverage
- Comprehensive coverage
- Liability coverage
- Deductible
- Premium
- Homeowners insurance
- Umbrella policy
- Renters insurance
- Health insurance
- COBRA
- Disability insurance
- Life insurance
- Face value
- Beneficiary
- Term life insurance
- Permanent life insurance
- Estate
- Estate planning
- Will
- Executor
- Intestate
- Trust

Objectives

When you complete Chapter 6, you will be able to:

- **Describe** property insurance including related liability coverage.
- **List** various types of health insurance plans.
- **Discuss** life insurance and other types of insurance coverage that are available.
- **Explain** how estate planning involves insurance, wills, and trusts.

Chapter 6 Insurance: Protecting Your Assets

Your Financial IQ

Before you read this chapter, answer the following questions to see how much you already know about insurance.

1. If you drive, how much is your car insurance?

2. Do you know what an underinsured motorist is?

3. What is a deductible and how does it affect what you pay for insurance?

4. You are involved in a car accident and everyone is okay. What should you do next?

5. How do you think that the insurance company assesses the value of your property in the event of fire or theft?

6. What is renters insurance?

7. If someone breaks into your house and steals property, do you know what to tell the insurance company?

8. Have you ever purchased extended warranty insurance?

9. Explain what you know about health insurance coverage.

10. Do you need life insurance if you are single? Why or why not?

Property Insurance

Life is full of risks. A **risk** is the possibility that an unfavorable situation could happen to you or something you own. Such an unfavorable situation often results in loss—financial or otherwise. The loss could be due to damage or theft of property. For example, your car could be damaged in an accident or your house could be destroyed in a fire. Whenever possible, you should avoid or reduce risk. For example, driving your car responsibly and within the speed limit helps you reduce the risk of an accident.

Insurance is protection you purchase against financial loss. There are many types of insurance you will need to think about as an adult. Insurance is a very important part of your financial plan. Insurance costs a lot of money, so you must think about how much you need and can afford. Then you can build the costs into your budget.

Car Insurance

If you are of driving age, you are probably familiar with car insurance. Car insurance provides protection against financial loss related to your car. For example, your car could be damaged in an accident or stolen. The policy may also protect you if you damage someone else's property or injure someone with your car. Car insurance is required in most states.

You probably already know that automobile insurance can be very expensive for anyone under age 25. In addition to age, other factors that will influence how much you pay include:

- Gender
- Driving record
- Insurance claims you have made
- Where you live
- Credit record
- Marital status
- Type of car

You may get a better rate if you are included on the policy of a parent or guardian. Getting good grades and taking driving classes may also reduce your insurance costs. If you are thinking about purchasing a car, research the cost of insurance for the car you want before you buy it. Typically, the sportier the car, the more insurance will cost. Consider the cost of the insurance as part of the cost of the car. You may reconsider the type of vehicle you decide to buy.

When you search for car insurance, you can "pick and choose" the coverage you buy as shown in Figure 6-1. As you can see, there are many choices in determining the car insurance that is right for you. Do not spend more on car insurance than you actually need, but make sure you are adequately covered.

F.Y.I.
A safe-driving course may lower your car insurance premiums up to 10%.

Figure 6-1 Types of Car Insurance Coverage

Type	Coverage
Property liability	Covers damage you do to others' property if an accident is your fault.
Bodily injury liability	Covers injury to other persons, including medical bills and lost wages if an accident is your fault.
Uninsured/underinsured motorist	Covers your medical expenses if the person who caused the accident does not have insurance or does not have enough coverage, or if you're a victim of a hit and run. Required in some states.
Collision	Covers your auto if damaged regardless of which party was responsible.
Comprehensive	Covers damage to your car caused by something other than an accident such as fire, theft, or vandalism.
Medical	Covers medical treatment for you and your passengers if you are in an accident regardless of fault.
Roadside assistance	Covers the cost if your car breaks down and needs to be towed.
Rental reimbursement	Covers cost of a rental car for a short time if your vehicle is damaged or stolen.

Collision coverage pays for damage to your car from an accident. If you have a newer car, you will want to have collision insurance to repair or replace your car. However, if you are driving a clunker that is 10 years old, collision insurance may not be necessary. **Comprehensive coverage** pays for damage unrelated to a collision. For example, your car might be stolen or damaged in a fire. Most states require you to have **liability coverage**. It protects those you may injure or whose property you may damage. Always be sure to protect yourself with liability coverage. You don't want to take a chance on a lawsuit by someone injured as a result of your driving.

The **deductible** is the amount you will pay before your insurance company pays a claim. Deductibles can range from $250 to $1,500. The higher the deductible, the lower your premium will be. A **premium** is the amount you pay for the insurance. You may be able to lower the cost of your insurance if you raise the deductible. For example, you could change it from $250 to $500 or more.

Insurance companies let you pay your premium annually, semiannually, quarterly, or monthly. If you spread your payments over months or quarters, the insurance company will usually charge an extra fee. So be sure to calculate how much additional money you will pay if you choose not to pay in one lump sum. These decisions will have an impact on your budget.

Auto Insurance Application

Complete the following form for auto insurance. This exercise will be good practice for when you are ready to apply for insurance.

Personal Auto Application			
Insured Information			
Driver's Name:			
Driver's License Number:			
Date of Birth:			
Marital Status:	Single ☐	Married ☐	Divorced ☐
Home Address:			
City:	State:		Zip:
Phone Number:			
Fax Number:			
E-mail Address:			
Vehicle Garaging Address:			
Prior Coverage Information			
How Long Have You Had Continuous Coverage?			
Prior Carrier Name:			
Prior Policy Number:			
Limits of Insurance			
Liability Limits for Per Vehicle/Per Accident:	25/50 ☐	50/100 ☐	100/300 ☐	250/500 ☐
Combined Single Limit:	100,000 ☐	300,000 ☐	500,000 ☐
Property Limit (Your Vehicle):	$		
Comprehensive Deductible:	250 ☐	500 ☐	1,000 ☐
Collision Deductible:	250 ☐	500 ☐	1,000 ☐
Vehicle Information			
Vehicle Year:			
Vehicle Make and Model:			
Vehicle License Number:			
VIN Number:			
Odometer Reading:			
Annual Mileage:			

http://www.endlessinsurance.com/thankyou.html

Chapter 6 Insurance: Protecting Your Assets

Example 6-1

Your car insurance premium is $375 if paid annually. If you pay semiannually, you pay $190; quarterly, $100; monthly, $35. What is the annual cost for each option? How much more will you pay if you pay monthly rather than once a year?

Step 1 Calculate semiannual premium

Semiannual premium	$190.00
Number of payments in year	× 2
Annual premium	$380.00

Step 2 Calculate quarterly cost

Quarterly premium	$100.00
Number of payments in year	× 4
Annual premium	$400.00

Step 3 Calculate monthly cost

Monthly premium	$35.00
Number of payments in year	× 12
Annual premium	$420.00

Step 4 Calculate the difference

Premium paid monthly	$420.00
Premium paid annually	− 375.00
Difference in cost	$45.00

You Do the Math 6-1

Your car insurance premium is $295 if paid annually. If paid semiannually, the premium is $150; quarterly, $82.50; monthly, $32.25. What is the annual cost for each option? How much more will you pay if you pay monthly rather than once a year?

Step 1 Calculate semiannual premium

Semiannual premium	_____
Number of payments in year	_____
Annual premium	_____

Step 2 Calculate quarterly cost

Quarterly premium	_____
Number of payments in year	_____
Annual premium	_____

Step 3 Calculate monthly cost

Monthly premium _____

Number of payments in year _____

Annual premium _____

Step 4 Calculate the difference

Premium paid monthly _____

Premium paid annually _____

Difference in cost _____

F.Y.I.

If you "total" your car (damage it beyond repair), your insurance company may pay the "blue book" value of the car. This amount might not be what you think it is worth. The term "blue book" refers to the Kelly Blue Book, which lists car values.

Check Your Understanding

What is the purpose of car insurance?

_____
_____
_____

Auto Insurance

1. Each state requires different types and amounts of car insurance for drivers. Use the Internet to find the legal requirements for your state and list them below.

_____
_____
_____
_____

2. Has your state adopted no-fault insurance? If so, explain how it works.

_____
_____
_____
_____

Chapter 6 Insurance: Protecting Your Assets

3. Search the web for several different auto insurance companies. Find the approximate premiums for at least five different makes and models of cars. At least one should be your "dream" car—the brand-new car you would buy if you had the money. At least one should be a very affordable car—not necessarily this year's model. Also determine the cost of the premium for each car if you pay semiannually, quarterly, or monthly. Assume you want full coverage and have a $500 deductible.

Car	Premiums			
	Annual	Semiannual	Quarterly	Monthly

4. Using the same cars, break down the cost of premiums based on collision, liability, and comprehensive coverage. Would you be able to save some of the premium cost by eliminating some coverage?

Car	Collision	Liability	Comprehensive

5. Now look up the blue book value for the same five cars.

Car	Blue Book Value

Dollars and $ense

Know your Auto Insurance Policy

Including money for insurance is an important part of financial planning and creating your budget. At your age, you will probably be most interested in car insurance. While in school, you might be on your parent's or guardian's car insurance policy. If you are, have your parent or guardian explain the coverage on you and your car. It is important for you to understand what is covered and your responsibilities as a driver.

- ❑ Do you have an insurance card in the glove compartment of your car?
- ❑ Do you have the phone number of your insurance company?
- ❑ Is a copy of the title to the car in the glove compartment?
- ❑ Are there pen and paper in the glove compartment in the event that you need to write down any information if an accident should happen?

As you become independent and responsible for your own car insurance, you will have to budget for your insurance payments. It is important that you have proper coverage and that you have the ability to pay the premiums on time. You should never drive a car without insurance.

Talk with someone with experience who can guide you on the types of coverage you will need for your car. Check your budget and see how much you can afford to spend for insurance. Then shop around and talk with several insurance companies to see what types of rates they offer.

Homeowners Insurance

Homeowners insurance covers a house and its contents. Typically, it also provides liability coverage for when someone is injured (think ice-covered sidewalk, for example) at your home. You will not be able to obtain a mortgage to buy a home unless you have proof of insurance on the house. Make sure the insurance covers the cost of replacing the house, not what you paid for it. The contents should be covered at their current market value.

Contents in a home include furniture, appliances, linens, clothing, TVs, and other items. Contents are usually insured for a minimum of 50% of the value of the house. However, if you have a lot of expensive items, you may need a higher coverage. It is a good idea to keep an inventory of household and personal items. You should update it regularly. Your insurance company may give you a booklet to keep an inventory of the items.

Your policy may also pay for the cost of staying someplace else if your home is damaged. For example, you might not be able to live in your home safely while it is being repaired after a fire. Once again, the higher the deductible, the lower your premiums will be.

Example 6-2

Your home is insured for $285,000. You want to make sure you have enough coverage on the contents, so you opt for 65% on the contents. How much coverage will you have on the contents of your home?

Value of home	$285,000.00
Percent coverage for contents	× .65
Coverage on contents	$185,250.00

You Do the Math 6-2

You insure your home for $190,000. You have several big screen TVs and a lot of computer equipment, so you insure the contents for 60% of the home's value. How much coverage will you have on the contents?

Value of home	_____
Percent coverage for contents	_____
Coverage on contents	_____

Check Your Understanding

What is the advantage to paying one annual premium for homeowners insurance?

_____

_____

Umbrella Policies

Many families have an umbrella policy. An **umbrella policy** covers losses above the limits of your other policies. You may have $1 million or more in protection. The term "umbrella" refers to shielding you more broadly than primary coverage. Typically, this type of policy goes into effect only when all other policies have paid their full amounts. Umbrella coverage can also provide protection for claims that are not covered by other policies. These claims might be for libel or slander, for instance.

Check Your Understanding

Why would someone want to purchase an umbrella insurance policy?

_____

_____

Renters Insurance

When you rent an apartment, the property owner's insurance covers the building itself. It does not cover your possessions that are in your apartment. You might be surprised when you total the value of your belongings. You might have furniture, TVs, and computers. Jewelry, clothes, and other household items add to the list. These items would be expensive to replace if they were damaged or stolen.

Many apartment complexes require you to have renters insurance. **Renters insurance** covers you for theft or damage to the contents of your apartment. It also provides liability coverage for when someone gets hurt in your apartment. For example, someone could be injured by slipping and falling on a wet floor.

While you are away at college, you may be covered by your parent's or guardian's policy. This may be the case whether your items are in a dorm room or a rented apartment. Renters insurance is not expensive, and its coverage is definitely worth the cost.

Some policies pay the depreciated value of the lost items. Other policies cover replacement costs. When you buy renters insurance, make sure your policy pays replacement costs.

Check Your Understanding

Do you need renters insurance if the owner of your apartment building has insurance on the building? Why or why not?

_____
_____
_____
_____

Health and Disability Insurance

Health insurance is protection against financial loss due to illnesses or injuries. Medical costs can be very expensive. So having health insurance is important. Some employers pay part of the cost of health insurance for employees. If you can get health insurance through your employer, it will probably be cheaper than buying an individual policy on your own.

COBRA stands for the Consolidated Omnibus Budget Reconciliation Act. This act requires that you be allowed to continue health care provided through your employer after you have been laid off or have voluntarily left your job. The coverage can be extended for up to 18 months. You will have to pay the full premium for this coverage, so it will be costly. However, it enables you to have extended health care until you arrange to be covered under another plan.

There are three main types of health insurance plans. These plans are discussed in the following sections.

F.Y.I. Most young people can be covered under their parents' health insurance through age 26.

Inventory

1. Assume you will be going away to college or renting your own apartment soon. Make a list of items you will be taking. Give an approximate replacement cost for each item. Include furniture, clothes, computers—everything that you think you will take with you.

Item	Replacement Cost

2. Total the value of all items. Then contact an insurance agent or do research online to get an estimate of how much your renters insurance premium would be.

HMO Plans

HMOs are a popular type of health insurance plan. HMO stands for *health maintenance organization*. With an HMO, you mainly use doctors, hospitals, and clinics in the HMO's network. A referral may be needed if you have to see a specialist. You may not be covered if you receive care from a doctor that is not in the network. Be sure to look over the list of doctors carefully. Is your family doctor on the list? What about specialists that you see? If you are unsure whether the doctors you have been seeing are part of the plan network, ask them. HMOs are often less expensive than other types of plans.

PPO Plans

PPOs are another type of health insurance plan. PPO stands for *preferred provider organization*. PPOs have a network of doctors and hospitals that you can use. The insurance company has agreed with these providers upon reduced rates. You will usually have a small co-payment per visit. You can also use others doctors and hospitals that are not in the network. If you use providers that are not in the network, however, your costs will be higher. A PPO is a more flexible plan than an HMO.

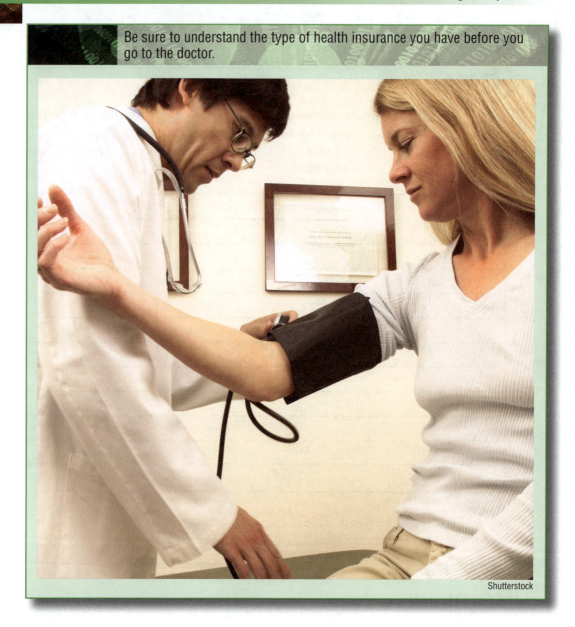

Be sure to understand the type of health insurance you have before you go to the doctor.

POS Plans

POS plans are another common type of health insurance. POS stands for *point of service*. With a POS plan, you select a primary care physician from a list of those in the network. This person supervises your care and refers you to specialists if needed. You may not have to pay a co-payment if you see the doctors within the plan network. Co-payments and deductibles are higher if you see doctors outside the plan.

If you buy health insurance through your employer, you may not have a choice in the plan that is offered. However, you will probably pay more if you choose to buy health insurance on your own. Health insurance plans can be very confusing. You should ask a lot of questions before you select a plan. With any of the plans, you may have to pay a percentage of the cost if you are hospitalized. Know what your deductibles are, if any, and what your co-payments will be.

F.Y.I.
Nonsmokers may get a discount on health insurance.

Chapter 6 Insurance: Protecting Your Assets

Many plans offer some type of coverage for prescription drugs. Many people have no clue what medicines cost. They simply pay a co-payment of $10, $15, or $20 and do not think about the total cost of the drug. The cost may be as much as $50 to $150 or more for a 30-day supply. If it is available to you, select a plan with prescription coverage.

Example 6-3

Your employer withholds $25 each week from your paycheck for health insurance premiums. Your plan requires a $10 co-payment for each doctor visit, and a $15 co-payment for prescription medicines. If you visit your doctor three times this month and have to fill two prescriptions, what is your total medical expense for the month?

Step 1 Calculate your health insurance premiums

Weekly premiums	$25.00
Number of premiums	× 4
Monthly insurance premium	$100.00

Step 2 Calculate doctor co-payments

Doctor co-payment	$10.00
Number of visits	× 3
Total doctor co-payments	$30.00

Step 3 Calculate prescription co-payments

Prescription co-payment	$15.00
Number of prescriptions	× 2
Total prescription co-payments	$30.00

Step 4 Calculate monthly medical costs

Monthly premiums	$100.00
Doctor co-payments	30.00
Prescription co-payments	+ 30.00
Total monthly cost	$160.00

You Do the Math 6-3

You pay $52.50 semimonthly for health insurance premiums. Your plan requires a $20 co-payment for each doctor visit and a $15 co-payment for prescription medicines. If you visit your doctor twice this month and need four prescriptions, what is your total medical expense for the month?

Step 1 Calculate your health insurance premiums

Semimonthly premiums	_____
Number of premiums	_____
Monthly insurance premium	_____

Step 2 Calculate doctor co-payments

Doctor co-payment _____

Number of visits _____

Total doctor co-payments _____

Step 3 Calculate prescription co-payment

Prescription co-payment _____

Number of prescriptions _____

Total prescription co-payments _____

Step 4 Calculate monthly medical costs

Monthly premiums _____

Doctor co-payments _____

Prescription co-payments _____

Total monthly cost _____

Medical Accounts

Some businesses offer employees the opportunity to contribute to an HSA (health savings account). Contributions to this type of medical account are tax deductible. You won't pay taxes on this money as long as it is used for medical expenses. HSA funds are used for medical expenses not covered by your insurance. For example, the money could be used for deductibles and co-payments. You can roll over unspent funds to the following year.

Other businesses offer employees an opportunity to enroll in a FSA (flexible spending account). This is very similar to the HSA account with contributions that are tax deductible. The main difference in these accounts is that you must use funds in an FSA account before the end of the plan period—usually by the end of the year. If all the funds are not used, you will lose the amount that is unused.

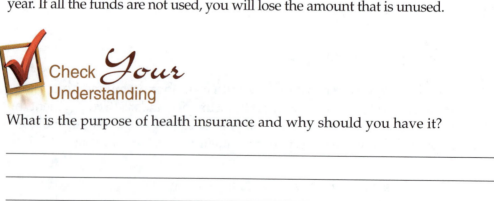

What is the purpose of health insurance and why should you have it?

_____

_____

Health Savings Accounts

Search the Internet to find options in your state for Health Savings Accounts or Flexible Spending Accounts. List at least three things you find about each type of account.

HSA Accounts

1. _____
2. _____
3. _____

FSA Accounts

1. _____
2. _____
3. _____

Disability Insurance

Once you are supporting yourself, you should think about disability insurance. **Disability insurance** pays a portion of your income if you are injured or ill and cannot work. These plans typically pay 50% to 70% of your wages or salary. However, there may be a waiting period of 30 to 60 days before coverage begins. This is one more reason to have that six month's cash reserve! You may be able to buy disability coverage through your employer.

Do not confuse disability insurance with workers' compensation. Every state requires employers to have workers' compensation insurance. This pays benefits when you are injured on the job. If you are injured elsewhere or become ill, you will not be covered by workers' compensation.

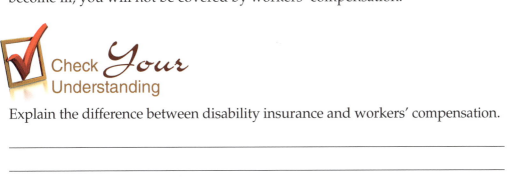

Explain the difference between disability insurance and workers' compensation.

_____
_____
_____

Life Insurance

Most young people don't think of life insurance until they become adults. Once you have a spouse, children, or others who depend on your income, life insurance coverage is very important. **Life insurance** provides benefits after your death to persons you have selected.

Life insurance premiums are based on age, health, occupation, and hobbies. In other words, if you go mountain climbing every weekend, your premiums will be higher than someone whose hobby is stamp collecting. The younger you are, the less expensive life insurance is likely to be.

The **face value**, or death benefit, is the amount payable upon your death. A **beneficiary** is a person you have named in your policy to receive the benefits. You can name more than one person if you wish. For example, a young single adult might name parents or siblings as beneficiaries. A married person might name a spouse or children. Amounts received from life insurance policies are generally not taxable. There are two basic types of life insurance: term insurance and permanent life insurance.

Term Life Insurance

Term life insurance is a policy that provides coverage only for a specific period of time. The term might be for five years or ten years, for instance. Term insurance is the cheapest and most basic form of life insurance. How much you need, of course, will vary according to your financial responsibilities.

When you get a full-time job, your employer may offer low-cost group term life insurance. The premium for term insurance is typically low when you are a young person. However, the cost may increase as you get older. The policy may terminate if you switch jobs. Some policies have a clause that guarantees you can renew the policy—usually at a higher rate. Term insurance is often used as protection when taking out a loan to insure the debt will be repaid if the borrower dies.

Term insurance may be the most affordable type of life insurance for you to purchase on your own. Make sure your policy is renewable without a physical exam. Also, be sure that you have the option of converting it to permanent insurance. This option is usually offered within the first several years that you have the policy.

Permanent Insurance

Permanent life insurance is a policy that lasts for the life of the individual. Typically, you will pay a fixed premium for as long as you live and have the policy. The insurance company will pay a set death benefit when you die. Permanent life insurance grows in cash value. This means that you will receive some money if you cancel the policy. The amount depends on how long you have had the policy and its terms. Various names for these policies are whole life, universal life, and variable life.

Having permanent life insurance eliminates the worries a person might have with term insurance. You will be covered as long as you pay the premiums, no matter what your health status may be. The cash value may build up enough to pay the premiums as you get older. So you will continue to be covered with little or no out-of-pocket premiums. This is a big advantage over term life insurance.

You may cancel a permanent life insurance policy in order to receive its cash value. You may also be able to withdraw part of the cash value or request the cash value as a loan. The death benefit will be reduced by the amount you withdraw. The death benefit is restored when a loan is paid in full. The company will charge you interest to borrow against your policy. However, the loan may provide needed cash in an emergency. The interest rate should be lower than credit card interest.

Permanent policies may also give you the option of receiving a monthly income. This income is called an annuity. This money can help you pay expenses during your retirement.

F.Y.I. As with health insurance, non-smokers may pay less for life insurance.

Check Your Understanding

Explain the purpose of life insurance and the various types that are available.

_____
_____
_____
_____

Insurance Plan

What is your insurance plan for the next several years? List the types of insurance you think you will need and what each will cost.

Type of Insurance	Cost

Other Insurance

We have talked about several types of insurance, but there are many more available for you to buy. Remember that you want to be insured, but not over insured. It is important that optional insurance premiums fit into your budget. Here are some other types of insurance you may want to review in the future.

- Warranty insurance on appliances, cars, and other assets that you purchase. Think carefully when asked if you want to purchase this type of insurance. The cost of the coverage may be more than the value of the item you are purchasing.
- Dental and vision insurance cover costs related to your teeth and eyes. This insurance is good to have if it is cheap enough and fits in your budget.
- Flood insurance is required if your home is in a designated flood plain.
- Travel cancellation insurance covers losses if you have to cancel and the expenses are not refundable. Flight insurance may be included free if you charge airline tickets on your credit card.
- Disease coverage pays if you develop a specific disease such as cancer. However, this type of insurance isn't necessary if you have adequate health insurance.
- Long-term care insurance pays if you are confined to a nursing home, an assisted-living facility, or need in-home care.
- Pet insurance covers veterinary expenses for pets.

Think about how much insurance you really need and the premiums you can afford. Then select the plans that are right for you.

Estate Planning

As with insurance, estate planning is probably not on your mind right now. You may not even know what the term means. In a few years, however, you may have a career and a family. You will want to think about planning for your and their financial welfare. Your **estate** is your net worth—the value of your assets minus your debts. **Estate planning** is the process of arranging your financial affairs so that your wishes will be followed now and after your death. Part of your estate planning should include life insurance because its proceeds are tax-free. However, other investments and assets left to your heirs may be taxable.

Wills

A **will** is a legal document that states who you want to receive your assets when you die. Wills can be drawn up inexpensively. There are even online programs you can use to create a will. However, the will should be signed in the presence of witnesses. It is important that a will list your beneficiaries and a guardian if you have children. Many wills also appoint a guardian for pets.

A will also names an **executor**. This person will manage your estate and be sure your wishes are carried out. The executor is usually a trusted family member or friend. However, it could be an officer of a bank or other financial organization. In this case, the executor would be entitled to a fee.

Many people think that because they are not wealthy, they have no need for a will. If you die **intestate** (the legal term for not having a will), the state will decide who gets your property. The state will also decide who gets custody of dependent children under 18 years of age. Do not leave such important decisions to the state or the courts.

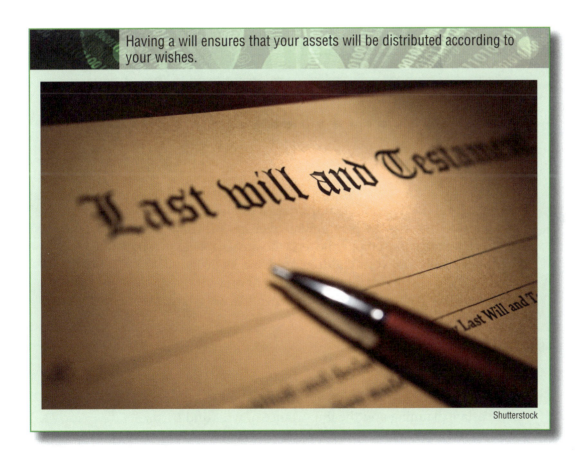

Having a will ensures that your assets will be distributed according to your wishes.

Shutterstock

Inheritance Laws

1. Go online and research what the law is in your state if you die intestate. List in order the distribution of assets.

   1. _____
   2. _____
   3. _____
   4. _____
   5. _____

2. Pretend you are going to write a will today. Make a list of your assets that you would include in your will.

   _____
   _____
   _____
   _____
   _____
   _____

Trusts

A trust can be created along with your will to help manage your assets. A **trust** is a legal document that authorizes a trustee to manage your estate on your behalf. A trustee is the person who oversees the trust. A trust is useful if you have young children or children who are unable to manage money. You can declare that all your children reach a certain age, such as 25, before the trustee divides your estate among them to prevent the money from being squandered. Trusts are used especially when there is a large estate involved.

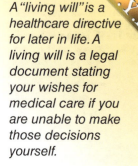

A "living will" is a healthcare directive for later in life. A living will is a legal document stating your wishes for medical care if you are unable to make those decisions yourself.

Check Your Understanding

Explain estate planning and the importance of wills and trusts.

_____
_____
_____

Chapter 6 Insurance: Protecting Your Assets

Looking to Buy Insurance
A Checklist

Young adults need to begin thinking about insurance. There are so many kinds of insurance available; it is sometimes challenging to decide what is most important. Use this checklist to help you consider insurance.

Yes	No	
____	____	1. Do I understand what risk means and why it is important to have insurance?
____	____	2. Do I know how much my car insurance costs and how often I must pay it?
____	____	3. Do I know what my car insurance covers?
____	____	4. If I move into an apartment, do I know how much renters insurance will cost?
____	____	5. Do I have an inventory of my personal items that would need to be replaced in the event of a theft or fire?
____	____	6. Will I be covered by someone's health insurance until I am 26?
____	____	7. Do I have dental insurance?
____	____	8. Do I have vision insurance?
____	____	9. Do I have a life insurance policy?
____	____	10. Do I have a job or plan for paying for insurance that I purchase when I graduate from high school?

Chapter Review

Summary

Insurance is protection you purchase against financial loss. It should be an important part of your financial plan. Property insurance is available for cars and homes. These plans provide coverage for damage or theft as well as liability protection. An umbrella policy covers losses above the limits of your other policies. Health insurance is protection against financial loss due to illnesses. Disability insurance pays a portion of your income if you are ill and cannot work. Medical costs can be very expensive, so having health insurance is important. Life insurance provides benefits after your death to persons you have selected. Estate planning is the process of arranging your affairs so that your wishes will be followed now and after your death. Your estate planning may include life insurance as well as wills and trusts.

Review Questions

Circle the correct answer for each of the following.

1. Automobile insurance that pays for damage to your car in an accident is called
   A. liability coverage.
   B. collision coverage.
   C. comprehensive coverage.
   D. premium coverage.

2. The amount you pay after a car accident before your insurance pays is called
   A. deductible.
   B. liability.
   C. premium.
   D. comprehensive.

3. Automobile insurance that pays for damage if your car is stolen is called
   A. liability coverage.
   B. collision coverage.
   C. comprehensive coverage.
   D. premium coverage.

4. Insurance that covers your personal possessions in an apartment is called
    A. liability insurance.
    B. premium insurance.
    C. homeowners insurance.
    D. renters insurance.

5. A health savings account
    A. allows you to make tax-free contributions.
    B. allows you to roll over unspent funds to the next year.
    C. can be used to pay medical expenses.
    D. All the above.

6. A type of insurance that pays benefits to replace part of your income if you are unable to work because of illness or accident is called
    A. health insurance.
    B. disability insurance.
    C. comprehensive insurance.
    D. liability insurance.

7. The face value of a life insurance policy is the same as the
    A. death benefit.
    b. premiums.
    c. beneficiary.
    d. cash value.

8. The type of life insurance that covers you for a set period of time is called
    A. whole life insurance.
    B. variable life insurance.
    C. term life insurance.
    D. universal life insurance.

9. A legal document that states how your assets are to be distributed upon your death is called a(n)
    A. PPO plan.
    B. will.
    C. insurance plan.
    D. estate.

10. Someone who is designated to carry out your wishes in distributing your estate upon your death is called a(n)
    A. executor.
    B. intestate.
    C. premium.
    D. beneficiary.

Build Your Vocabulary

For each word or term, write the correct definition using your own words.

11. Risk

12. Insurance

13. Premium

14. Liability coverage

15. Homeowners insurance

16. Umbrella policy

17. Life insurance

18. Beneficiary

19. Permanent life insurance

20. Estate planning

21. Will

22. Trust

Apply Your Math Skills

Calculate the answers to the following problems.

23. Your car insurance premium is $236 if paid annually. If you pay semiannually, you pay $125; quarterly, $65; monthly, $25. What is the annual cost for each option? How much more will you pay if you pay monthly rather than once a year?

24. Your home is insured for $223,000. You want to insure the contents for 55% of the home's value. How much coverage will you have on the contents?

25. You pay $37.25 semimonthly for health insurance premiums. Your plan requires a $15 co-payment for each doctor visit, and a $20 co-payment for prescription medicines. If you visit your doctor three times this month and require five prescriptions, what is your total medical expense for the month?

7
Education: A Passport to Your Future

Terms

Academic degree
Community college
Proprietary school
Trade school
Reserve Officers' Training Corps (ROTC)
529 plan
Grant
Scholarship
Work-study programs
Need-based awards
Lifelong learning
Professional development
Mentor
Seminar

Objectives

When you complete Chapter 7, you will be able to:

- **Describe** the importance of a career.
- **Discuss** various options for higher education.
- **List** various ways of funding higher education.
- **Explain** the importance of lifelong learning.

Chapter 7 Education: A Passport to Your Future

Your Financial IQ

Before you read this chapter, answer the following questions to see how much you already know about getting an education after high school.

1. What is the difference between a university and a community college?

2. How long is typically required to earn an associate's degree, a bachelor's degree, and a master's degree?

3. Why would someone attend a trade school?

4. Explain the difference between a community college and a proprietary school.

5. What is a scholarship, and how is one earned by a student?

6. Can you get an education by enrolling in the military?

7. What are some ways to finance a college education?

8. Explain the difference between a scholarship and a grant.

9. How does a student qualify for financial aid?

10. What is meant by *lifelong learning*?

Your Career

Have you thought about what you will do when you finish high school? The choice you make will have a huge impact on your life. You probably have been thinking about "what I want to be when I grow up" for most of your life. Now, you will be making decisions as to what that career will be.

Choosing the right career isn't only about money. It is also about values and what will make you content with what you are doing. As you think about potential careers, your counselor can help you research careers that interest you. Your counselor will also be able to give you aptitude tests and career assessment tests. These tests help match your skills with a career that may be suitable for you.

As you are researching careers, you will want to learn about opportunities for employment in careers that interest you. What are the employment trends in this occupation—will the need for your career expand in the future or decline? How much can you expect to earn in your chosen career? You will want to find answers to these questions. This is an exciting time of your life and the opportunities are endless!

Career Choices

1. Use a printed copy of *The Occupational Outlook Handbook* or access the *Handbook* online. Read about five career options that you find interesting.

2. Read about careers that are projected to grow quickly in the United States during the next few years. (In the printed *Handbook*, look for Overview of the Projections. If you are working online, search using the term *fastest growing careers*.) List below five of those careers that you might be interested in pursuing.

   _____
   _____
   _____
   _____
   _____

3. Choose the career you are most interested in and write a short report. In the report, include:
   - The career or job name
   - The employment outlook
   - Training and education necessary
   - Any certifications needed
   - Salary or wages for the career

Check Your Understanding

What are two questions you should research about careers that interest you?

___

___

Higher Education

Do not underestimate the value of an education. Getting an education can help you increase your future wealth and advance in your chosen career. Funding for your education should be a big part of your financial plan. You need to start making these plans now.

College or University

The value of education is measured in terms of the personal benefits as well as the financial benefits that it may bring. One advantage of a college education is that it enables you to be a well-rounded person. You can choose from many areas of interest. At college, you may meet people from your state or from around the world. Whether you go to a local college or one across the country, you will become more aware of the diversities throughout our nation.

There are many colleges and universities from which to choose. There are many degrees that can be earned. An **academic degree** is an award given to a person by a college or other school. It signifies that the person has successfully completed a course of study. An associate's degree can usually be earned in two years. In four years, a bachelor's degree can typically be earned. A master's degree typically requires one or two years after earning a bachelor's degree.

How much money do college graduates make compared to high school graduates? A report from the U.S. Census Bureau deals with this question. According to the report, earning power greatly increases with a college degree. The typical college graduate earns much more per year than a high school graduate does. Review the numbers shown in Figure 7-1.

F.Y.I. *Most people will change careers several times during their working years.*

Figure 7-1 Annual and Lifetime Earnings

	High School Graduate	Some College	Associate's Degree	Bachelor's Degree	Master's Degree	Doctoral Degree	Professional Degree
Annual Earnings	$30,400	$36,800	$38,200	$52,200	$62,300	$89,400	$109,600
Lifetime Earnings	$1.2 million	$1.5 million	$1.6 million	$2.1 million	$2.5 million	$3.4 million	$4.4 million

Source: The Big Payoff: Educational Attainment and Synthetic Estimates of Work-Life Earnings; U.S. Census Bureau, http://www.census.gov/prod/2002pubs/p23-210.pdf.

Example 7-1

Suppose you graduate from college and make $23,000 more each year than a high school graduate. How much more than a high school graduate will you earn in your lifetime if you work a total of 45 years?

Amount per year	$23,000.00
Number of years worked	× 45
Difference in earnings	$1,035,000.00

You Do the Math 7-1

Over your lifetime, your earnings are $27,500 more each year as a college graduate than your friend who is a high school graduate. If you both work a total of 43 years, how much more will you earn?

Amount per year	_____
Number of years worked	_____
Difference in earnings	_____

The additional earnings are more than a $1 million in each case. That seems like a pretty good reason to pursue higher education—right? The same report reveals that a person with a master's degree typically earns about $400,000 more in a lifetime than the person with a bachelor's degree. Of course, the higher your degree the more your earnings should be. These, of course, are average figures and depend on the state of the economy.

Example 7-2

In your lifetime, if you earn $400,000 more with a master's degree than you would with a bachelor's degree, how much more would you earn per year if you work 40 years?

Difference in earnings with master's degree	$400,000.00
Number of years worked	÷ 40
Annual difference in earnings	$10,000.00

You Do the Math 7-2

In your lifetime, your earnings are $415,500 more with a master's degree than they would be with a bachelor's degree. If you work a total of 45 years, what is the difference in your earnings per year?

Difference in earnings with master's degree	_____
Number of years worked	_____
Annual difference in earnings	_____

Chapter 7   Education: A Passport to Your Future   169

According the numbers in Figure 7-1, how much more does a person with a bachelor's degree typically earn per year than a high school graduate?

_____

_____

Wages

1. Go to the Bureau of Labor Statistics website. Search for wages by areas and occupations. Select a link to find data by state. Select your state.
2. List six careers in the table below. Record the average annual earnings in your state for each career.

Career Title	Average Annual Earnings

Two-Year Schools

Have any of your friends attended a community college? **Community colleges** are two-year schools. They offer academic or occupational programs. Some students choose to live at home and attend a local community college for a couple of years. Then they go to a four-year college to complete a degree. Credits earned from a two-year state college usually can be transferred to a four-year school.

There are also two-year **proprietary schools** which are privately owned institutions. They offer various programs and degrees. Examples include courses in business, modeling, paramedical training, and tax preparation. Self-improvement classes are also often offered. If you attend a proprietary school, make sure that the school is accredited. Also, check to see whether the credits you earn will transfer to a four-year school. If the credits will not transfer, you will have to retake those classes if you go to another college.

F.Y.I.
There are many schools that offer classes online. Always do a background check to make sure the school is legitimate. The United States Distance Learning Association (USDLA) is a good source of information.

Trade Schools

Trade schools are another form of higher education. **Trade schools** focus more on skills than academics. They are sometimes called *vocational schools* or *career and technical colleges*. Trade schools can prepare you for careers such as art/design/fashion, massage therapy, criminal justice, auto technician, nurses' assistant, plumber, electrician, and many more. Do not discount these schools. Many of them have smaller classes and better teacher/student ratios than big colleges. Sometimes they cost much less than a college. For those who do not want to spend four years in school or may not have the funding for college, trade schools may be a good option. Be aware that credits from a trade school generally will not transfer to a four-year college should you decide to continue your education there.

Vocational schools can prepare you for a career in many different trades.

Shutterstock

Military

Most branches of the U.S. Armed Forces offer the chance to earn a tuition-free college degree. They also provide opportunities to see the world. If you join the military, you will receive a salary, housing, and health care. Of course, you will be required to serve active or reserve duty.

Reserve Officers' Training Corps (ROTC) is a military program on many college campuses. It provides leadership training for commissioned officers. Graduates of ROTC become officers in a branch of the military, such as the U.S. Army or the U.S. Air Force. ROTC offers a wide variety of education and training programs with little or no cost to you. ROTC programs are on many college campuses. There may be a Junior ROTC program in your high school. If you are interested in serving in the military, check out this program.

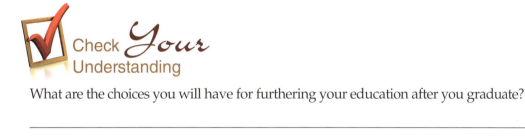

Check *Your* Understanding

What are the choices you will have for furthering your education after you graduate?

_____
_____
_____
_____

Funding Your Education

As you are making decisions about schools, you will need to create a financial plan for paying for your education. Whether you attend a trade school or university, someone has to pay the cost of the education. Figure 7-2 shows potential sources of funding for higher education.

You may be fortunate enough to have a 529 plan to fund your college education. A **529 plan** is a savings plan for education. It is generally operated by a state or college. These funds may be used for qualified colleges across the nation. Plans vary from state to state. Each state now has at least one 529 plan available. However, not all states offer tax incentives for 529 plans. Research the features and benefits of a plan before you invest. There are restrictions on how this money can be used. You will be penalized if you use money invested in a 529 plan for anything other than education expenses.

Many students who have to pay for all or part of their education work their way through school. You should begin planning how you will pay for your education now. There are many college calculators online that can help you estimate how much money you will need to fund your education.

Figure 7-2 Sources of Funding

Potential Sources of Funding	Conditions/Repayment
Scholarships	No repayment. May qualify for academic, sports, music, dance, or other areas—including school mascots.
Grants	No repayment. Issued by government agencies, corporations, states, and other organizations.
Work-study programs	Paid jobs typically backed by government agencies. Apply on campus.
Bank loans	Must be repaid, usually at a higher interest rate than government college loans.
Internships	Career-based jobs. You may or may not be paid, but it may count as college credit. Provides work experience.
529 plan	Savings plans for setting aside money to send students to college. Sponsored by states or colleges.
Military enlistment	Provides education, training, and opportunity to see the world. Typically require active or reserve duty.
Government education loans	Must be repaid. Repayment may be postponed until you begin your career. Have lower interest rates than regular bank loans. Many options are available. Talk to your school counselor for information or go online.

Financial aid is available from the federal government and other sources. The Federal Student Aid program provides more than $100 billion in grants, loans, and work-study assistance each year. Some states also offer college money to attend a state school if you have good grades in high school.

- A **grant** is usually provided by a nonprofit organization (such as the government). Money from a grant does not have to be repaid. Grants are typically based on need and are usually tax exempt. Grants may also be provided by a corporation or a foundation. You may have heard of Pell grants, which are available to students with low family incomes. Cost of the college and your status as a full-time student affect the award. These grants may be used at almost any college. A FAFSA application for a Pell grant should be available at your high school and can be accessed online.

- A **scholarship** may be based on financial need or some other type of merit or accomplishment. Some scholarships are based on ACT or SAT scores. Others relate to grades, extracurricular activities, athletics, music, and other things. Many scholarships and grants go unused because no one has applied for them. Do not fail to apply for help just because you do not want to write an essay or fill out an application. Talk to your school counselor to learn whether you might qualify for scholarships. Meet all deadlines for applying.

> **F.Y.I.** Use student loans or other college money for the necessities of college—not for having a good time while you are there. College loans can take a lifetime to repay.

Chapter 7   Education: A Passport to Your Future

College Budget

In Chapter 3, you created a budget. When you get ready to go to college, you will need to create a college budget. Remember that fixed expenses are those that occur regularly and variable expenses are those that may change from day to day.

1. Based on your own spending experiences, estimate the amount you think your living expenses would be for the first month of college. Enter the amounts in the table that follows. Indicate if each expense is fixed or variable. (This will not include tuition, housing, or books.)

Living Expenses for College			
Expense	**Amount**	**Fixed**	**Variable**
Cell phone			
DVD rentals			
Music purchases			
Gas for the car			
Car insurance			
Movie tickets			
Three meals a day			
Haircuts			
Gifts			
Clothes			
Eating out with friends			
Other entertainment			
Sports clothing/equipment			
Personal care items			
Miscellaneous (list)			
Monthly Total			

2. What will be the total expenses for one semester (1 month x 4)?

3. What will be the total expenses for one year (1 semester x 2)?

4. If your expenses remained the same, how much would you spend over a two-year period?

5. If your expenses remained the same, how much would you spend over a four-year period?

- **Work-study programs** are usually part-time jobs on campus. These jobs are often funded by the school or government.
- **Need-based awards** are available for some students. Typically, the student must show financial need. Funds for these awards come from governments, school, and other groups or organizations.

Costs for School

1. Research at least three colleges, universities, or trade schools that you would consider attending. Then complete the costs for one semester.

Semester Number One					
Name of School	Tuition for One Semester	Books for One Semester	Dorm Expenses for One Semester	Total for One Semester	Total for One Year (Two Semesters)

2. If costs remained the same, how much would you spend over a two-year period?

3. If costs remained the same, how much would you spend over a four-year period?

As you are making the decision on where to go for an education, consider all your options. Is it worth it to spend $40,000 to $50,000 or more per year to go to a private school? Maybe not, in terms of lifetime earnings. Be sure to investigate state or local colleges where you can make your money go farther. You can still earn a degree whether you live on campus or stay at home (to save money). The experience of living away from home may give you a taste of freedom and responsibility. However, there may be some benefits of attending a prestigious college or private school. For example, you may have an advantage when looking for a career.

Example 7-3

You want to attend a private college in another state to obtain a bachelor's degree. However, your family wants you to attend a local college to save money. The private school would cost $42,500 per year. The local college would cost $5,800 per year if you live at home and commute. Assume that no help is available in scholarships or grants for either school. Calculate the difference in cost of attending the private college rather than the local college.

Step 1 Calculate the cost of private college

Private college cost per year	$42,500
Number of years	× 4
Total cost for private college	$170,000

Step 2 Calculate the cost of local college

Local college cost per year	$5,800
Number of years	× 4
Total cost for local college	$23,200

Step 3 Calculate the difference in cost

Total private college cost	$170,000
Total local college cost	− 23,200
Difference in cost	$146,800

You Do the Math 7-3

You want to attend a private college away from home for your bachelor's degree. Your friend is going to stay home and commute to a local college. The private college would cost $46,250 each year. The local college would cost $6,175 per year. No help is available in scholarships or grants for either college. Calculate the difference in cost of attending the private college rather than the local college.

Step 1 Calculate the cost of private college

Private college cost per year _____

Number of years _____

Total cost for private college _____

Step 2 Calculate the cost of local college

Local college cost per year _____

Number of years _____

Total cost for local college _____

Step 3 Calculate the difference in cost

Total private college cost _____

Total local college cost _____

Difference in cost _____

Check Your Understanding

List five options for funding your higher education.

_____
_____
_____
_____
_____

Funding

1. Make an appointment with your school counselor. Find out what scholarships, grants, or other funding may be available to you.
2. Enter the information in the table below so that you can use it as a guide for applying for funding. Add additional opportunities that you find that are not listed in this table.

	Funding Sponsors	Amount Available	Application Deadline
Work-study programs			
Scholarships			
Grants			
Financial aid			
Student loans			
Other			

Dollars and $ense

College Access

Have you heard the term *college access*? College access means gaining access to a school to continue your education after high school. The school could be a college, university, or trade school. Preparing to go to college presents many challenges to students and families. Having good grades and finding the money to pay for college are two of them.

Going to college is a big step for your future and an important part of your financial plan. The sooner you begin planning, the better—it is never too early. As you plan for your education, you will want to do research as much as possible to find out how to prepare academically as well as financially.

Make the most of your remaining high school years by doing the very best you can. Become involved in organizations at your high school or in your community. Colleges are looking for well-rounded individuals that take part in a variety of activities.

There are many websites that provide information to help you from the time you are in grade school until you apply for college. Each state offers resources. Do a search on *college access* for your state to find information. If you have already been thinking about a specific college, check their website to see if you will qualify and to find out what financial help might be available to you.

- ❑ The College.gov website is a great resource. It discusses why to go, what to do, and how to pay for college. Access the site at www.college.gov.
- ❑ The College Board offers a financial calculator to help project the cost of an education. Access the site at http://apps.collegeboard.com/fincalc/efc_welcome.jsp.
- ❑ The National College Access Program Directory provides information on post-secondary schools. You can get specifics about them and their offerings. Access the site at www.collegeaccess.org/accessprogramdirectory/.

If you have not already done so, talk to your family, friends, and counselors for information today to begin planning for college.

Lifelong Learning

Lifelong learning is a term that describes acquiring new skills and knowledge throughout your life. Learning may be for your career, for general knowledge in daily living, or for your personal interests.

Learning for Your Career

Improving or gaining new skills related to work is called **professional development**. When you graduate from college or a technical school, you should have the skills you need to begin your career. However, technology and methods of doing work can change rapidly. You may need to take classes to update your skills or learn new ones. Some employers pay for the cost of this training, also called continuing education. Careers in nursing, teaching, accounting, auto repair, and many other areas require that you have the latest training in order to keep your job.

In addition to taking classes, you can learn new skills and knowledge in other ways. Some companies provide on-the-job training. This training teaches workers to use new equipment or procedures. You may also learn from a mentor at work or in a professional association. A **mentor** is someone who has knowledge and skills and shares them with you, usually on an informal basis. Seminars are another good source of information. A **seminar** is a meeting or conference for exchanging ideas or learning new things. Some seminars are free or cost less than more formal classes at a school.

Learning for Daily Living

You are constantly being educated through the experiences of daily living. The media, your friends, family, and other sources provide new information. Some of this new information comes to you with little effort on your part. For example, a friend tells you about a sale at a local store where you can save money on the new TV you are planning to buy. For other learning, you may need to put forth some effort. For example, you may do research to learn about a company in which you want to invest money as part of your financial plan. You may read articles about political candidates when deciding for whom you will vote. You may need to read the product manual to learn how to program a new DVD recorder. You may visit travel sites on the Internet when planning a vacation. You will need to continue learning for daily living throughout your lifetime.

Learning for Personal Interests

As an adult, you may want to read books or articles, watch DVDs, or attend classes or seminars related to your personal interests. Personal enrichment classes are generally designed for your enjoyment. They help you learn something new or improve skills. For example, suppose you will be traveling to a foreign country and do not know the language. You may want to take a language class. Maybe you always wanted to play the piano or guitar. You could take piano or guitar lessons. Whatever your interests are, there are probably ways to learn more about them. Reading, enrolling in courses of interest, and attending seminars should all be a part of your lifelong learning.

Explain the idea of lifelong learning.

_____

_____

_____

Financial Aid Application

Completing applications to take entrance tests, apply for financial aid, and other forms requires a lot of information. For practice, complete the application for financial aid that follows.

Date: _____

APPLICATION FOR FINANCIAL ASSISTANCE

STUDENT INFORMATION:

Applying for: Fall 20 ____   Spring 20 ____   Summer 20 ____

Student Status: ☐ Prospective Student   ☐ Current Student   ☐ Undergraduate Student   ☐ Graduate Student

1. Name: _____
             Last   First   Middle   Maiden

2. Permanent Mailing Address: _____
             Number   Street   Apartment/Box #   Home Phone Number

   _____
         City   State   Zip Code   Cell Phone Number

3. E-mail Address: _____
4. Will you complete the Free Application for Federal Student Aid (FAFSA)?   ☐ Yes   ☐ No
5. Where do you plan to live during the academic year?   ☐ On-campus   ☐ Off-campus   ☐ With parents
6. Are you the beneficiary of a 529 prepaid tuition or 529 college tuition savings plan?   Yes   No
7. Are you currently employed?   ☐ Yes   ☐ No   ☐ Full-time   ☐ Part-time
8. Do you plan to work while in school?   ☐ Yes   ☐ No   ☐ Full-time   ☐ Part-time

ELIGIBILITY FOR SCHOLARSHIPS:

9. You may be eligible for a scholarship based on ethnicity or major. Providing the following allows you to be considered for these.

   Ethnic Background: _____   Anticipated Major: _____

10. Please indicate if you will be applying for any of the following types of aid/scholarships:
    ☐ Art   ☐ Debate   ☐ Music   ☐ Theatre   ☐ Work-Study   ☐ Loans

FINANCING YOUR EDUCATION:

11. Please indicate other sources of financial help (by amount) that you will draw upon for assistance this academic year:

    ☐ Personal Savings   ☐ Educational Loans
    ☐ Family Assistance   ☐ Personal Loans
    ☐ Earnings from Work during School Year   ☐ Government Benefits
    ☐ Educational Grants   ☐ Tuition Assistance from Employer
    ☐ Private Scholarships   ☐ Other

UNUSUAL CIRCUMSTANCES:

12. Families occasionally experience unusual expenses/circumstances beyond their control. If you believe such circumstances should be considered in determining your financial aid award, contact the Financial Aid Office for the appropriate forms.

Student Signature _____   Date _____

Being Financially Responsible

Preparing for Your Education
A Checklist

As you start planning for your education after high school graduation, you need to complete some specific tasks. This checklist is only a starting point and you should expand it as your research progresses. It is never too early to start planning for life after graduation, so start now.

Yes	No	
____	____	1. I generally focus on getting good grades. Good grades can help me get scholarships and be accepted into the school of my choice.
____	____	2. I have checked with my counselor to make sure I have taken/am taking the courses necessary to be accepted into a post-secondary institution.
____	____	3. I will take the PSAT, SAT, ACT, and AP exams when applicable.
____	____	4. I have practiced completing college entrance applications and financial aid applications. These forms require time and information, so practice is necessary.
____	____	5. I have created a file to keep certificates of awards, report cards, and other items that show my accomplishments. I may have to include these when I apply for college.
____	____	6. I participate in school and community activities. Most colleges expect students to have participated in a variety of school activities as well as volunteer work.
____	____	7. I have taken an aptitude or career assessment test to see how my skills and talents may influence my career choice.
____	____	8. I have researched various schools to see which one is suitable for my needs.
____	____	9. I have visited campuses to see what each school offers and how specific programs match up to my interest and needs.
____	____	10. I have created a plan to pay for my education. A plan may include loans, financial aid, working, or other resources.

Chapter Review

Summary

The career choices you make will have a huge impact on your life. You will want to learn about opportunities for employment in careers that interest you. Getting an education can help you increase your future wealth and advance in your chosen career. Higher education can be acquired from a college or university, a two-year school, a trade school, or through the military. As you are making decisions about schools, you will need to create a financial plan for paying for your education. You may receive some funds from grants, scholarships, loans, or work-study programs. Lifelong learning is a term that describes acquiring new skills and knowledge throughout your life. Learning may be for your career, for general knowledge in daily living, or for your personal interests.

Review Your Knowledge

Circle the correct answer for each of the following.

1. To help match your skills with a career that may be suitable for you, you could
   A. take an aptitude test.
   B. take a career assessment test.
   C. talk with a counselor.
   D. All the above.

2. A college degree that typically takes four years to complete is a(n)
   A. associate's degree.
   B. bachelor's degree.
   C. master's degree.
   D. doctorate degree.

3. A college or university
   A. offers only two-year programs.
   B. typically offers degrees in only one or two subject areas.
   C. typically offers degrees in many subject areas.
   D. does not award academic degrees.

4. Schools that focus more on skills than academics are called
   A. trade schools.
   B. vocational schools.
   C. technical colleges.
   D. All the above.

5. ROTC is a military program
   A. offered at many high schools.
   B. that provides leadership training for commissioned officers.
   C. that is not available at colleges.
   D. that does not offer education and training.

6. College assistance that is based on merit, such as high grades or musical talent, is called
   A. a grant.
   B. financial aid.
   C. ROTC.
   D. a scholarship.

7. Grants for funding your education
   A. do not have to be repaid.
   B. have to be repaid.
   C. are provided only by government agencies.
   D. are not provided by government agencies.

8. Options for funding higher education include
   A. loans.
   B. grants.
   C. work-study programs.
   D. All the above.

9. A method of funding higher education that requires that the money be repaid is a
   A. loan.
   B. grant.
   C. work-study program.
   D. All the above.

10. Professional development is
    A. learning new skills related to your personal interests.
    B. improving or gaining new skills related to work.
    C. learning new information for use in daily living.
    D. All the above.

For each word or term, write the correct definition using your own words.

11. Academic degree

_____

_____

12. Community college

13. Proprietary school

14. ROTC

15. 529 plan

16. Grant

17. Scholarship

18. Work-study program

19. Need-based awards

20. Lifelong learning

21. Mentor

22. Seminar

Apply Your Math Skills

Calculate the answers to the following problems.

23. Your earnings are $26,250 more each year as a college graduate than your friend who is a high school graduate. You both work 46 years. What is the difference in your earnings?

   _____

24. A worker's total earnings for 46 years are $422,750 more with a master's degree than they would be with a bachelor's degree. What is the difference in earnings per year between a master's degree and a bachelor's degree for this worker?

   _____

25. You want to attend a private school away from home for your bachelor's degree. However, your family wants you to attend a local college. The private school would cost $47,800 each year for four years. The local college would cost $5,985 each year for four years. No help is available in scholarships or grants for either school. How much could you save by attending the local college for four years?

   _____

8 Loans: Cars and Housing

Terms

Depreciation
Unsecured debt
Secured debt
Collateral
Installment loan
Car lease
Lessee
Lessor
Security deposit
Apartment lease
Mortgage
Equity
Foreclosure
Private mortgage insurance (PMI)
Escrow account
Fixed rate mortgage
Amortization
Adjustable rate mortgage (ARM)
Homeowners association (HOA) fee
Assessment

Objectives

When you complete Chapter 8, you will be able to:

- **Describe** the difference between obtaining a loan for a car and leasing a car.
- **Explain** the difference between renting a living space and buying a home.

Your Financial IQ

Before you read this chapter, answer the following questions to see how much you already know about transportation and housing.

1. Is a car an investment?

2. Does the price of a car affect the cost of insurance?

3. What is a secured debt?

4. Describe an installment loan and its purpose.

5. What is an upside down or underwater loan?

6. Why would you lease a car instead of buying a car?

7. When you lease a car, who pays the insurance?

8. What is a security deposit?

9. Why would you get a mortgage?

10. What does it mean when a lender forecloses on property?

Your First Car

If you are 16 or older, you may already have purchased your first car. If so, which car did you choose—the newest model sports car or a late model used car? Did you check to see how much you would pay for the insurance before buying that car?

As you know, car ownership brings with it huge financial responsibility. Not only do you have to pay to get the car, you have to pay insurance and maintenance costs to keep the car running. When you buy a car, you will also pay sales tax, a title fee, and a registration fee. You need to be prepared for these expenses as well as the monthly payment for a car.

In Chapter 9, you will learn about investments. Hopefully, the investments you make will *appreciate* (or increase) in value. However, this is not the case with money you use to buy a car. Do not think of a car as an investment. As soon as you drive the car off the lot, it starts losing value. This decrease in the value of an asset is known as **depreciation**. Think carefully about the kind of car you want. In some cases, it may make more sense to buy a used car rather than a new one. You may even want to lease a car rather than buy one.

Getting a Car Loan

As you create your financial plans, loan payments will probably be a part of your expenses each month. Many people will not pay cash for large items, such as cars or homes. They will get a loan to finance these purchases. Loans for an automobile may be for up to five years. A loan for a house may extend over 30 years.

There are two types of loans that are usually obtained by consumers—secured and unsecured. **Unsecured debt** is a promise to pay that is not backed by any specific asset. Credit card debt (Chapter 5) is unsecured. You can borrow money or purchase goods or services by just signing your name. You are, however, legally obligated to pay these unsecured debts.

Secured debt is backed by collateral, such as a car or home. **Collateral** is property accepted as security for a debt. The lender gets the property if you do not repay the loan. For example, suppose you get a loan for your car. You sign an agreement saying that if you do not make your payments, the lender can take your car. Secured debt is usually available at lower interest rates than unsecured debt because the bank can take something of value if you do not repay the loan.

Car loans are a type of installment loan. An **installment loan** is a purchase that is paid for in equal monthly payments. When you apply for an installment loan, the process will be very similar to the process of getting a credit card as described in Chapter 5. You will fill out an application and the lender will review your credit history to see if you are a good risk.

F.Y.I.
Repossession of a car means the lender can reclaim the car if you fail to make your payments. The car is not legally yours until the debt is completely paid.

Car Loan Application

1. Write a paragraph describing why you may need a car while in high school. Write another paragraph describing why you may need a car when you go to college.
2. Completing applications to get a car loan, credit card, and other forms take a lot of information and practice to get them right. For practice, complete the following application for a car loan.

CAR LOAN APPLICATION FORM

Name: _____
            First   Middle   Last

Address: _____
        Street   Apt #   City   State and Zip

Phone: _____
          Daytime   Evening   Cell

Date of Birth: __ __ / __ __ / __ __ __ __   E-mail: _____

Employer: _____ Title: _____ Phone: _____

Length of time at job: _____ Salary (hourly wage): _____ Monthly gross income: _____

Own or rent home: ☐ Own ☐ Rent Monthly payment: _____ Total monthly expenses: _____

Loan Type: ☐ Used car ☐ New car Loan amount: $ _____ Term 1 / 2 / 3 years

Down payment amount: $ _____ Do you have a cosigner available? ☐ Yes ☐ No

Have you filed for bankruptcy in the past seven years? ☐ Yes ☐ No Please explain: _____

Status: ☐ Single ☐ Married ☐ Separated ☐ Divorced

Permission for electronic fund transfer: ☐ Yes ☐ No

Financial References

	Bank/Institution	Account Number
Checking Account		
Savings Account		

Permission to Obtain Consumer Credit Report

By signing this application form, I hereby give the company the right to obtain a consumer credit report regarding me for this application and the loan should the application be approved.

I certify that the above information is correct to the best of my knowledge.

Applicant Signature _____ Date _____

Chapter 8   Loans: Cars and Housing

While getting your first car can be an exciting experience, it is also a huge responsibility.

Make sure you read the contract carefully before signing for an installment loan. Contracts should indicate the total amount of interest that you will pay over the loan period. The contract should state that there is no "prepayment penalty." This allows you to pay off the loan at any time without paying extra fees. The contract should also allow you to pay extra money each month. The extra amount should reduce the principal so that you can pay off the loan early.

Regardless of the type of your loan, secured or unsecured, you must make the payments on time. Failing to repay your loans will lower your credit score. Having a loan is an important responsibility and should be taken seriously.

 Check *Your* Understanding

Which type of loan, secured or unsecured, carries more risk for the lender? Why?

_____
_____
_____
_____

When you apply to get a loan for a car, you will have options as to how many years the loan will extend. Should you finance the car for two, three, four, or five years? Some dealers now offer loans for 72 months (six years) to finance a new car. Of course, the longer the time, the lower the monthly payments will be. However, the longer the time, the more interest you will pay.

In addition to the price of the car, you will pay tax and fees when you buy a new car. You will probably pay a destination fee in the amount of $300 to $600. The car dealer pays this fee to have the car delivered to the dealership site. This cost is passed on to you. You will pay sales tax at the rate set for your state on the purchase price including any options you select. You may also have to pay sales tax on the destination fee. You will pay DMV (Department of Motor Vehicles) fees to license and register your new car. These fees vary by state. They may be about 1% to 1.5% of the price of the car. Take a look at the math in the following example.

Example 8-1

You purchase a car for $18,750, which includes a destination fee of $400. Your state sales tax is 6%. The DMV fees are 1.2% of the price of the car. What is the total you must pay?

Step 1 Calculate the sales tax

Price of the car	$18,750.00
Sales tax percentage	× .06
Sales tax amount	$1,125.00

Step 2 Calculate the DMV fee

Price of the car	$18,750.00
DMV fees percentage	× .012
DMV fees amount	$225.00

Step 3 Total the amounts

Price of the car	$18,750.00
Sales tax amount	1,125.00
DMV fees amount	+ 225.00
Total amount	$20,100.00

You Do the Math 8-1

You purchase a car for $21,890, which includes a destination fee of $350. Your state sales tax is 7%. The DMV fees are 1% of the price of the car. What is the total you must pay?

Step 1 Calculate the sales tax

Price of the car _____

Sales tax percentage _____

Sales tax amount _____

Step 2 Calculate the DMV fee

    Price of the car   _____

    DMV fees percentage   _____

    DMV fees amount   _____

Step 3 Total the amounts

    Price of the car   _____

    Sales tax amount   _____

    DMV fees amount   _____

    Total amount   _____

There may also be an opportunity to trade your current car for another car. Sometimes this is a good deal, sometimes it is not.

Now that you have calculated the total cost of the car, can you afford the car? Will you need a car loan to pay part of the cost? You can do an Internet search for a car loan calculator. You can enter the amount of a car loan and see the monthly payments you will have to make. Your payment will be an important part of your budget. Using the example above, if we financed the entire amount of the car, the monthly payment would be $465.63 as shown in Figure 8-1. So before you get a loan for a car, make sure you can make those monthly payments. Four years is a long time to pay on a car.

Figure 8-1 Financial Calculator

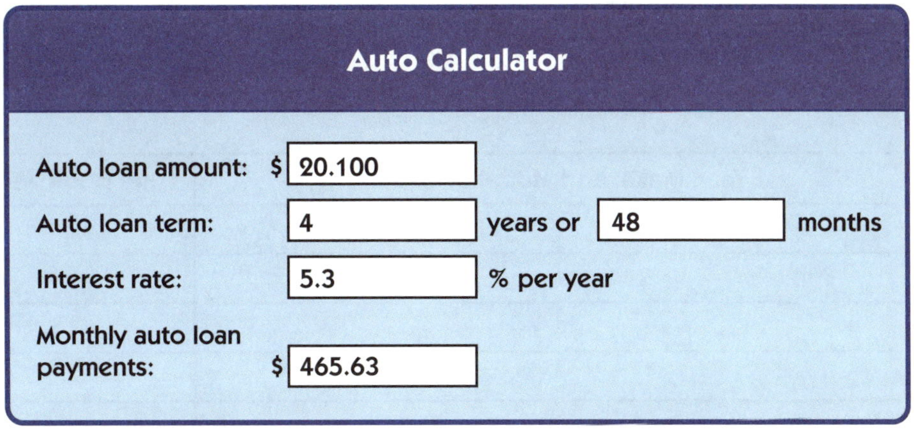

Auto Calculator

Auto loan amount: $ 20.100

Auto loan term: 4 years or 48 months

Interest rate: 5.3 % per year

Monthly auto loan payments: $ 465.63

Example 8-2

You want to trade in your old car valued at $2,750 on a new one. You look at a new car with a sticker price of $21,300. The dealer says he will take your old car in trade and give you a loan of $18,500. How much are you actually paying for the new car? Is this a good deal?

Loan amount	$18,500.00
Value of old car	+ 2,750.00
Cost of new car	$21,250.00

Note that this amount is $50 less than the sticker price of the new car.

You Do the Math 8-2

Your old car is valued at $4,850. You want to purchase a new car with a sticker price of $24,200. The dealer says he will take your old car in trade and give you a loan of $19,900. How much are you actually paying for the new car? Is this a good deal?

Loan amount	_____
Value of old car	_____
Cost of new car	_____

F.Y.I. If something happens to your car, the insurance company will only pay you the blue book value of the car. If you owe more than that, you will still have to pay the rest of your loan.

Car Values

1. Write the makes and models of five cars that either your family or friends own in the table below. The term *make* refers to the brand name of the car, such as Ford or Kia. The term *model* refers to the name of the particular car, such as Taurus.

Year, Make, and Model of Car	Blue Book Value

2. Go online and find the Kelly Blue Book value of each car. Write the amounts in the table.

The longer the time of the loan, of course, the more you will pay in interest. There is another factor to consider. If you finance a car for five or six years, you might owe more than the car is worth before you finish paying off the loan. Owing more than the value of any asset is called being *underwater* or *upside down* on the loan. If you think you need more than three years to pay off a car loan, you should probably look for a less expensive car.

Leasing a Car

You may decide not to purchase but to lease a car. What does it mean to lease a car? A **car lease** is a contract that allows you to use a vehicle in exchange for payment. When you lease a car, you are the **lessee** and the dealership is the **lessor**. The important thing to remember about leasing a car is that you are not making payments toward ownership. When leasing, you are making payments to use the car for a specific amount of time, usually two or three years. When you lease a car, you are responsible for insurance and maintenance, just as if you owned the car. You also will pay for the title and registration as well as sales tax.

There is usually a required down payment to lease a vehicle, generally $1,000 to $2,000. You may also have to pay a security deposit. A **security deposit** is an amount required by the dealer for assurance that the car will be in good condition when you return it. If you return the vehicle in good condition, you should get the security deposit back. You will not get back the down payment. When the lease is up, you may decide to purchase the vehicle. However, the cost may be higher than the car's blue book value. You might need a loan to finance the purchase unless you have enough money saved to buy it without a loan.

F.Y.I.
If you turn a leased car in before the lease is up, you will probably be charged an early termination fee. Such a fee would be stated in the lease contract.

Example 8-3

You decide to lease a vehicle for three years. The lease requires a down payment of $1,200 plus a security deposit of $500. You will make monthly payments of $300 for the three years. What is the total cost to lease the car for three years?

Monthly payments	$300.00
Number of months	× 36
Payments for lease	$10,800.00
Down payment	1,200.00
Security deposit	+ 600.00
Total cost	$12,600.00

Remember that you may receive your security deposit of $500 back at the end of the lease.

You Do the Math 8-3

You decide to lease a vehicle for two years. The lease requires a down payment of $500 plus a security deposit of $550. You will make monthly payments of $275 for the two years. What is the total cost to lease the car for two years?

Monthly payments	_____
Number of months	_____
Payments for lease	_____
Down payment	_____
Security deposit	_____
Total cost	_____

So should you buy or lease? Your age, job situation, and other factors will determine the better solution for you when the time comes to make a decision. The car dealer should be able to offer you different monthly payments depending on your down payment. Typically, the larger the down payment you make, the lower your monthly payments will be. Figure 8-2 shows a comparison of factors related to buying or leasing a car.

Check Your Understanding

Explain what it means to lease a car.

_____
_____

Figure 8-2 Buy or Lease Comparison

Factors	Purchase	Lease
Ownership of car	Purchaser	Company leasing the car
Auto license and title	Purchaser pays	Lessee pays
Sales tax (most states)	Purchaser pays	Lessee pays
Mileage limit	No limit	Limit per year plus cost per mile for going over
Insurance on car	Purchaser's responsibility	Lessee's responsibility
Maintenance	Purchaser's responsibility	Lessee's responsibility
Monthly payments	Loan payments may be higher than lease	Monthly payments may be less than car loan payments
End of term	Purchaser owns the car (when any loan is paid)	Lessee turns car back in at end of time—no ownership
Excessive wear and tear	Decreases the value of the car the purchaser owns	Lessee may be charged a fee

Chapter 8 Loans: Cars and Housing

Being Financially Responsible

Buying a Car
A Checklist

Getting a loan for your first car may be your first installment loan, and it will affect your credit rating. So treat the process with respect. Make sure the loan is one you can afford. How would you rate your "car personality"?

Yes	No	
___	___	1. I will look for dependability in a car instead of a new or sporty car.
___	___	2. I will make sure that I can make the payments before getting a loan.
___	___	3. I will do all the calculations on the cost of borrowing money to make sure I am getting the deal that works best for me.
___	___	4. I will have a cosigner available to sign with me for the loan.
___	___	5. I will shop around for the best interest rates for a car loan.
___	___	6. I will practice completing an application for a loan so I am prepared when I go to the bank to apply.
___	___	7. I will do my homework and calculate the cost of insurance before buying a car.
___	___	8. I will do my homework and calculate the car maintenance before buying a car.
___	___	9. I will do my homework and calculate the cost of gas before buying a car.
___	___	10. I will read the contract for the loan and make sure I understand each point.

Housing

Housing will play a major part in your financial plan. Whether you purchase a house or rent, you will spend a large part of your money for a place to live. If you buy a home, you will pay insurance, taxes, utilities, and maintenance of the property in addition to the mortgage payment. If you rent, you will probably pay utilities and renters insurance in addition to the rent payment.

F.Y.I. *Many people spend 30% to 35% of their paychecks for housing.*

Renting a Living Space

> **F.Y.I.**
> The renter is the lessee and the property owner is the lessor in an apartment lease.

As a young person, you will probably rent your first living space, rather than purchase a home. It is very exciting to be out on your own and rent your first apartment. When you rent your first place, you will probably sign an **apartment lease**. This contract outlines the conditions of the agreement to rent the apartment for a certain length of time, usually a year. The lease will probably state specifics such as those listed below.

- The term of the lease states how long you will rent the apartment under the agreement. Apartment leases generally are for one year.
- The monthly rent amount is stated. The lease will also state the day of the month your rent is due.
- The lease states that you will be responsible for the property and not cause any damages. If you do cause damages, you will have to pay to repair them.
- The amount of the security deposit and when it is due is stated in the lease. The deposit is usually due when the lease is signed. A security deposit is to assure the property owner that you will leave the property in good condition when you move out. A typical security deposit is equal to the amount of the first month's rent, but it may be more.
- The lease should state whether you are responsible for expenses such as utility hook ups and payments.
- The lease should state any restrictions on pets or whether they are allowed.

When you are in college or working at your first job, it may make sense to have a roommate to share your expenses. Remember to include renters insurance when planning for that first apartment.

Give It a Go

Renting an Apartment

Renting your first apartment will take a lot of research. You will need to determine if you have enough money to rent an apartment. You will also have to decide where you want to live. Make a list of ten things you need to consider before you start an apartment search.

1. _____
2. _____
3. _____
4. _____
5. _____
6. _____
7. _____
8. _____
9. _____
10. _____

Dollars and $ense

Renting Your First Place

Even though it now seems a long time away, before you know it, you will be renting your first apartment. You may rent an apartment because you are going to college in another town. Maybe you have landed your first job and are ready to live on your own. In either case, renting your first place will be fun. However, you should do a lot of planning to prepare for that first apartment.

The first thing you need to do is to create a budget. Remember how you created a budget in Chapter 3? It will be a good idea to create an "apartment budget" to guide you in what you can afford. You will list your fixed and variable expenses. Then you will determine how much money you have each month for apartment rent. This will take some time. Start working on your budget before you are ready to start looking for an apartment.

Remember that renting an apartment involves paying utilities, renters insurance, and other expenses that you have not had until now. Make sure you do your homework and know exactly how much money you will need.

Once your budget has been prepared, the apartment hunt can begin! After you have decided how much you can afford each month, the next important factor will be location. You will want to find a place that is close to school or work. Ideally, it will be in a safe neighborhood. The price must fit within your budget.

After you select a location, you can use the Internet, newspapers, and other resources to find places that are available for rent. Select four or five that sound good, and set up appointments to look at them. You will probably have a roommate. If so, it is important that you agree on a place that you like.

You may need to look at several apartments to find one you want to rent. Then you will need to fill out an application. The property owner will probably check your credit and ability to make monthly payments. Then you will hear whether your application to rent has been accepted. Read carefully and make sure you understand the lease before you sign it.

Before you start looking for an apartment, do an Internet search for "renting your first place." The articles you find should be helpful to you in your apartment search.

Buying a Home

The biggest investment for many people is a home. There are many reasons to buy a house. Financially, it is usually a wise decision. The value of your house, unlike your car, normally goes up over a period of years. The amount you owe on the mortgage goes down. A **mortgage** is a type of secured loan used for buying property. The difference between what you owe on your house and the current market value is called **equity**.

With a home mortgage, your home is the collateral for the loan. If you do not make the payments, the lender can repossess, or take your home away from you. **Foreclosure** is a process in which the lender takes possession of the house if you fail to make the mortgage payments.

> **F.Y.I.**
> When you buy a house, you may deduct the mortgage interest from your taxes as an itemized deduction. Interest on car loans, credit cards, and most other loans is not tax deductible.

Depending on where you live, the average cost of a small "starter" home could be well over $100,000. The average price of new homes sold in the United States in 2010 was $270,900. This data is from the U.S. Census Bureau. Prices vary depending on the area of the country. Traditionally, lenders have required 20% of the price as a down payment on a house. That would be $20,000 for a very modest $100,000 house.

It is possible to borrow more than 80% of the home's value. Some loans are available with only 5% down. However, with a down payment of less than 20%, you will probably be required to buy **private mortgage insurance (PMI)**. PMI is required by lenders to insure payment if the borrower defaults on the loan. PMI will add as much as $50 or more to your monthly payment, depending on the amount you borrow. To be allowed to discontinue the PMI, you must pay the loan down to 80% of the home's value and obtain a current appraisal.

When you buy a home, you will have to pay taxes on the home and property insurance premiums. Rather than pay each of these expenses once a year, you may choose to set up an escrow account. An **escrow account** is an account for holding money in trust for others. In this case, an account is set up by the lender for you. You pay part of your insurance and taxes each month along with your mortgage payment. That way, you save gradually for the cost of taxes and insurance instead of making a lump sum payment. The lender will then take this money and pay your taxes and insurance when they are due.

Check Your Understanding

Describe a home mortgage.

_____
_____
_____
_____

Fixed Rate Mortgage

When you borrow money to buy a home, you may get a fixed rate mortgage. A **fixed rate mortgage** is a secured loan with a rate that does not change. The term of the mortgage is usually either 15 or 30 years. However, the loan can be for other terms. Your monthly payments will stay the same until the loan is paid in full. Typically, you can pay off the loan early or make additional payments. However, the amount of your required payment will not go up.

Buying a house takes a lot of money. Your mortgage payment will consist of principal and interest. At the beginning of your mortgage loan, your payments will mostly go toward interest. Very little of the payment will reduce the principal. Even though your payment remains the same, the amount you pay toward the principal will gradually increase. The amount for interest slowly decreases. The process of making equal payments on a loan while reducing the principal is called **amortization**. You can find mortgage calculators online. These programs will

Chapter 8 Loans: Cars and Housing

help you determine what your payments will be and how much interest you will pay over the life of the loan. You will calculate amounts for paying interest and reducing the principal for one year of a loan in Example 8-4.

Example 8-4

Calculate the principal paid over the first year for a mortgage of $150,000 with an interest rate of 6%. Monthly payments are $900. Note that the payment is fixed, but the amount of your interest and principal changes each month.

Step 1 Calculate the amount of interest for the first month

Amount of loan	$150,000.00
Interest rate	× .06
Annual interest	$9,000.00
Number of months	÷ 12
First month's interest	$750.00

Step 2 Calculate the amount applied toward principal

Monthly payment	$900.00
Interest payment	− 750.00
Amount applied toward principal	$150.00

Step 3 Calculate the new principal balance for the second month

Amount of loan	$150,000.00
Amount applied toward principal	− 150.00
Principal for the second month	$149,850.00

Month	Beginning Balance	Yearly Interest	Monthly Interest Amount	Principal Reduction Amount	New Balance
1	$150,000.00	$9,000.00	$750.00	$150.00	$149,850.00
2	149,850.00	8,991.00	749.25	150.75	149,699.25
3	149,699.25	8,981.96	748.50	151.50	149,547.75
4	149,547.75	8,972.87	747.74	152.26	149,395.49
5	149,395.49	8,963.73	746.98	153.02	149,242.47
6	149,242.47	8,954.55	746.21	153.79	149,088.68
7	149,088.68	8,945.32	745.44	154.56	148,934.12
8	148,934.12	8,936.05	744.67	155.33	148,778.79
9	148,778.79	8,926.73	743.89	156.11	148,622.68
10	148,622.68	8,917.36	743.11	156.89	148,465.79
11	148,465.79	8,907.95	742.33	157.67	148,308.12
12	148,308.12	8,898.48	741.54	158.46	148,149.66
Totals			$8,949.66	$1,850.34	

You Do the Math 8-4

Calculate the principal paid for the first year on a mortgage of $135,000 with an interest rate of 5.75%. Monthly payments are $795.

Month	Beginning Balance	Yearly Interest	Monthly Interest Amount	Principal Reduction Amount	New Balance
1					
2					
3					
4					
5					
6					
7					
8					
9					
10					
11					
12					
Totals					

Buying a home usually has financial advantages over renting a living space.

Shutterstock

Chapter 8 Loans: Cars and Housing

Mortgage Payments

Set up a spreadsheet to calculate principal and interest payments for the first year of a $163,800 mortgage with an interest rate of 5.25%. The monthly payments are $905. Write the answers for the first year of payments.

Month	Beginning Balance	Yearly Interest	Monthly Interest Amount	Principal Reduction Amount	New Balance
1					
2					
3					
4					
5					
6					
7					
8					
9					
10					
11					
12					
Totals					

Adjustable Rate Mortgage

An **adjustable rate mortgage (ARM)** is a secured loan with an interest rate that can change periodically. The interest rate can go lower or higher based on market conditions. There may be a cap on the rate—a maximum interest rate. However, the interest rate for this type of mortgage can increase several percent over the life of your loan. This means that your monthly payment could go up to a payment that you cannot afford to pay. Many people got ARMs in the 2000s with very low initial interest rates. However, they were unable to continue making their payments when the rates went up. They lost their homes to foreclosure.

The housing market collapse in the 2000s happened for many reasons. One reason was that people got loans for more money than they could afford to repay. Then the economy changed. Many people lost their jobs and could no longer afford high monthly payments. Some homeowners were so far in debt that they had to walk away from their homes and let the lender foreclose. With the housing market collapse, the value of homes decreased. This meant that many homeowners owed more on their house than it was worth. (They were underwater.) You never want to be in a situation where you owe more on an asset than it is worth.

F.Y.I.

A mortgage with a fixed rate is preferable in most cases over an adjustable rate. With a fixed rate mortgage, your interest rate and payments are guaranteed not to increase.

Do a lot of research before buying a house. There are laws that protect the consumer from lender and seller abuse. If you have questions about loans, seek advice from a professional to learn about the laws that protect you as a consumer.

Be sure to have your emergency fund of three to six months' living expenses. Look at not only the house, but also the neighborhood, community, schools, churches, businesses, and the general area. You may be there a long time. Hopefully, the value of the house will increase and you will build equity.

Mortgage Calculator

You are a first-time homebuyer. You want to purchase a single-family house in your area that costs $185,000. You do not have a 20% down payment. You will make a $20,000 down payment. Assume you have good credit and you are not including taxes and insurance in your monthly payments. You want a fixed rate mortgage with a term of 15 or 30 years. Find an easy-to-use mortgage calculator online. Fill in the following table to compare payments with different interest rates.

Interest Rate	Monthly Payments Term 15 Years	Total Interest Paid	Monthly Payments Term 30 Years	Total Interest Paid
5%				
5.5%				
6%				
6.5%				
7%				

Note: Look at the full amortization schedule to see how much interest and principal you are paying on the first few years of payments. Very little of your payment in the early years goes to principal; most goes to interest.

Why is a fixed rate mortgage less risky for the borrower than an ARM?

_____
_____

Buying a Condo

If you choose not to rent an apartment or buy a house, buying a condo may be a good choice for you. A condominium (condo for short) is a form of property ownership. The buyer purchases a part of a structure rather than all of it. Think of a condo as an apartment that you buy rather than rent. You will pay your mortgage, taxes, insurance, and other expenses that are a part of home ownership.

Other people also own parts of the condo building or complex. As a group, all the owners make up the homeowners association. Each owner (member) is required to pay a **homeowners association (HOA) fee**. The fee might be paid monthly or yearly. This fee is for insurance, upkeep of the buildings and common areas, landscaping, snow removal, and other amenities. Fees are typically set by the HOA board of directors who are elected by the members. If the number of members is small, the entire group may vote on fees and other issues. Before you buy, consider these fees when determining whether you can afford your monthly payments.

There could also be additional assessments levied if the HOA needs money for large expenses. An **assessment** is an amount required by the HOA to pay for major expenses. For example, a new parking lot might be required or a building might need a new roof. Ask to see the records for the past several years to see if assessments are regularly imposed on members.

Example 8-5

Your condo mortgage is $595.75 per month. In addition, you pay another $35 for PMI and $83.50 for HOA fees. What are your monthly fixed condo expenses?

Mortgage payment	$595.75
PMI	35.00
HOA fees	+ 83.50
Total condo expenses	$714.25

Keep in mind that this amount does not include monthly expenses such as utilities, cable, phone, and other items related to your home.

You Do the Math 8-5

Your condo mortgage payments are $633.45 monthly. You pay $27.50 for PMI and $73.25 for HOA fees. What are your monthly fixed condo expenses?

Mortgage payment	_____
PMI	_____
HOA fees	_____
Total condo expenses	_____

Chapter Review

Summary

Owning a car or a home brings with it huge financial responsibility. Not only do you have to pay to get the car or home, you have to pay insurance and maintenance costs. For some people, leasing a car is a good alternative to buying one. Many people rent a house or an apartment rather than buying a house or condo. Many people will not pay cash for large items, such as cars or homes. They will get a secured loan to finance these purchases. You should consider the interest rate, term, any related insurance, and fees carefully when getting a loan to purchase a car or home. Be sure that you can afford the monthly payments. If you fail to make payments on a loan, the lender may repossess the car or foreclose on the home.

Review Your Knowledge

Circle the correct answer for each of the following.

1. The gradual decrease in the value of an asset is called
   A. repossession.
   B. foreclosure.
   C. appreciation.
   D. depreciation.
2. A type of debt that is backed by something of value is called
   A. unsecured debt.
   B. secured debt.
   C. underwater debt.
   D. PMI debt.
3. A car loan is an example of a(n)
   A. unsecured debt.
   B. mortgage.
   C. lease.
   D. installment loan.
4. When you lease a car, you are the
   A. renter.
   B. lessor.
   C. lessee.
   D. cosigner.

5. Owing more on an asset than it is worth is called being
   A. underwater on the loan.
   B. in equity.
   C. in assessment.
   D. in foreclosure.

6. A loan obtained when you purchase a home and use the home as collateral is a(n)
   A. unsecured debt.
   B. foreclosure.
   C. mortgage.
   D. assessment.

7. The difference between what you owe on your home and the balance of the mortgage on the home is called
   A. equity.
   B. assessment.
   C. foreclosure.
   D. underwater.

8. When a bank takes possession of a home because the borrower has failed to make loan payments, it is called
   A. underwater.
   B. mortgage.
   C. assessment.
   D. foreclosure.

9. An account for holding money in a trust for others is called a(n)
   A. mortgage.
   B. assessment.
   C. escrow.
   D. foreclosure.

10. A type of mortgage that allows the interest rate to change is called a(n)
    A. fixed rate mortgage.
    B. adjustable rate mortgage.
    C. underwater mortgage.
    D. collateral mortgage.

Build Your Vocabulary

For each word or term, write the correct definition using your own words.

11. Unsecured debt

   _____

   _____

12. Collateral

   _____

   _____

13. Car lease

14. Security deposit

15. Apartment lease

16. Private mortgage insurance (PMI)

17. Escrow account

18. Fixed rate mortgage

19. Amortization

20. Assessment

Apply Your Math Skills

Calculate the answers to the following problems.

21. You purchase a car for $24,400, which includes a destination fee of $300. Your state sales tax is 5%. The DMV fees are 1.5% of the price of the car. What is the total you must pay?

22. Your old car has a value of $1,800. You want to buy a new car with a sticker price of $19,750. The dealer says she will take your old car in trade and give you a loan of $17,900. How much are you actually paying for the new car? Is it a good deal?

___

23. You decide to lease a vehicle for three years. The lease requires a down payment of $1,500 plus a security deposit of $650. You will make payments of $325 for the three years. What is the total cost to lease the car for three years?

___

24. Calculate the principal paid over the first year on a mortgage of $143,500 with an interest rate of 5.5%. Monthly payments are $815. What is the total amount of interest paid for the year? What is the total principal paid for the year? What is the ending balance?

___

___

___

___

25. Your condo mortgage payments are $736.90 per month. You pay $35.80 for PMI and $100.00 for HOA fees. What are your monthly fixed condo expenses?

___

9 Investments: Making Your Money Work for You

Terms

- Investing
- Security
- Stock
- Common stock
- Preferred stock
- Dividend
- Stock market
- Fluctuations
- Recession
- Expansion
- Bull market
- Bear market
- Diversification
- Growth
- Stock split
- Mutual funds
- Bond
- Coupon rate
- Corporate bonds
- Municipal bonds
- U.S. savings bonds
- Investment portfolio
- Dollar-cost averaging

Objectives

When you complete Chapter 9, you will be able to:

- **Identify** the reasons investors buy stock.
- **Explain** the difference between mutual funds and individual stocks.
- **Describe** three categories of bonds.
- **List** other types of investments and discuss how you can begin investing now.

Chapter 9 Investments: Making Your Money Work for You

Your Financial IQ

Before you read this chapter, answer the following questions to see how much you already know about investments.

1. Explain what it means to own stock in a company.
   _____
   _____

2. Are stocks insured by the FDIC?
   _____
   _____

3. What is a bear market?
   _____
   _____

4. What does a person have to do to collect dividends?
   _____
   _____

5. What is a mutual fund?
   _____
   _____

6. Describe what a financial advisor's job is.
   _____
   _____

7. Why would a person buy government bonds?
   _____
   _____

8. When making investments, what does *diversification* mean?
   _____
   _____

9. Name two other investments, besides stocks and bonds, that people often make.
   _____
   _____

10. What is an investment portfolio?
    _____
    _____

Stocks

In Chapter 4, you learned about bank accounts and earning interest. Bank accounts are an important part of your financial plan. However, at some point you may be ready to invest. **Investing** is buying a financial product or asset in an effort to increase your wealth over time. Hopefully, when you invest money, your principal (the amount you invest) will grow.

One form of popular investments is known as securities. A **security** is a document that shows evidence of ownership or debt. The most common types of securities are stocks and bonds. Stocks are discussed in this section. Bonds are discussed later in this chapter. An investor buys securities expecting to make a profit without any further effort.

The term **stock** refers to a share of ownership in a company. Everyone who buys shares of stock is an owner of the company. This ownership entitles you to share in the company's profits. In earlier years, companies issued certificates of ownership to their buyers. Today, however, you are more likely to receive a registration statement when you purchase shares of stock. The sample statement in Figure 9-1 shows a purchase of shares of stock.

There are two basic types of stock—**common stock** and **preferred stock**. Common stock earns dividends when companies declare them. A **dividend** is a share of the company's profits received by stockholders. Common stockholders can vote at shareholder meetings on company policies and directors. Preferred stockholders have first claim on assets if the company fails, but they have no voting privileges. Preferred stock earns dividends when companies declare them.

> **F.Y.I.**
> Two of the world's largest stock exchanges are in New York and London, England. The New York Stock Exchange (NYSE) is located on Wall Street in New York City. Wall Street has become known as the financial center of the United States.

Figure 9-1 Stock Registration Statement

Buying Stocks

Stocks are bought and sold on a **stock market**, also called a stock exchange. Companies may sell stock as a way to raise capital (money) for the operation or expansion of the company. This buying and selling of stocks is commonly known as trading.

Chapter 9 Investments: Making Your Money Work for You

Many large companies whose names you recognize are public corporations. That is, they sell their stock to the public. Some very well-known companies, however, are privately held corporations. A privately held corporation has few stockholders (maybe just one), and its stock is not available for sale to the public.

Stocks are bought and sold on a stock exchange.

Research Corporations

In the first column of the table, list the names of five companies that you recognize. The companies could be clothing stores, fast-food restaurants, or other retail stores. Then go to the websites of these companies to determine whether they are public corporations or privately held corporations. Find at least one that is privately held.

Name of Company	Publicly or Privately Held
1.	
2.	
3.	
4.	
5.	

When you buy stock in a company, you can follow its progress by checking the stock quotes in the newspaper or on the Internet as shown in Figure 9-2.

Many people avoid buying stocks because they think doing so is too risky. There is, indeed, a risk in buying stocks. Savings accounts, money market accounts, and CDs are insured by the FDIC. However, investments are not insured. There is no guarantee that you will not lose your principal when you invest in the stock market. No government insurance will cover you for losses if your stock goes down in value. Buying stock is a calculated risk. In the long run, however, stocks typically outperform many other types of investments.

Your goal should be to buy stocks at a low price, and sell stocks when the prices are high. However, think of owning stock as a long-term investment—not a get-rich-quick scheme. Do not get excited and immediately sell if you see that stock prices go down or even up in value. Remember, owning stock is an investment designed to build value over a long term.

You are young and probably have many working years ahead of you. Be prepared to ride out **fluctuations**, or the ups and downs in the stock market. A **recession** occurs when stock prices fall and unemployment rises. Traditionally, the market has always recovered from downturns and recessions—even from the Great Depression of the 1930s. Historically, **expansions** (the upward trends in the stock market) have lasted a lot longer than recessions.

Market fluctuations are discussed in terms of bull and bear markets. A **bull market** means stock prices are rising. A **bear market** means that stock prices are falling or staying at a low level. The term *market correction* is sometimes used to describe a sudden change in the market. For example, stock prices may drop suddenly after a steady increase in prices.

> **F.Y.I.**
> How can you remember a bull market vs. a bear market? The bull walks with his horns up (prices upward). A bear walks with his paws down (prices downward).

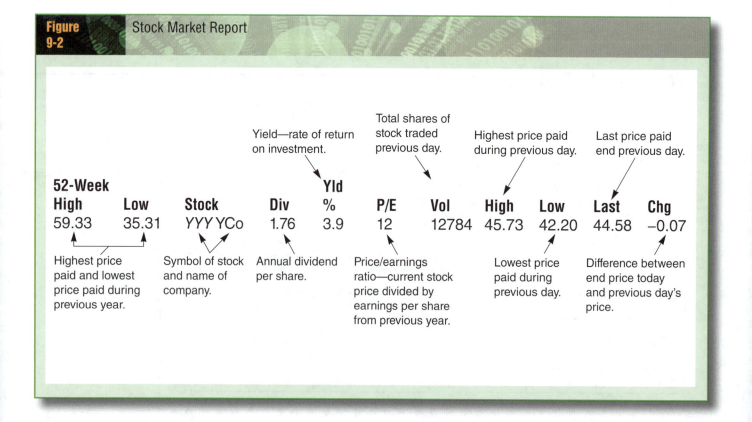

Figure 9-2 Stock Market Report

Stock Market Report

1. Write a paragraph describing the current state of the stock market. Is it a bear or bull market? Give facts to back up your opinion.

_____
_____
_____
_____
_____
_____
_____

2. Take a look at this stock market report and answer the following questions.

NAME	TICKER	CLOSE	CHG	52-WK RANGE LO	52-WK RANGE HI	WK CHG	YTD %CHG	DIV
AK Steel Hold	AKS	14.10	+.26	11.34	26.75	+1.08	-34.0	0.20
Air Transport Svcs	ATSG	7.95	+.13	1.78	7.86	+.36	+201.1	...
Am Financial Gp	AFG	31.83	...	23.26	31.88	+.86	+27.6	0.65f
Amylin	AMLN	13.12	+.15	9.51	24.21	+.02	-7.5	...
Ashland Inc	ASH	52.67	-.29	35.09	63.73	+1.12	+32.9	0.60
AtriCure Inc	ATRC	10.06	+.81	4.54	9.35	+1.44	+66.6	...
Bank of Kentucky Fin	BKYF	17.60	-.27	14.15	22.81	-.25	-6.3	0.56
CSX Corp	CSX	64.41	+.38	42.05	64.50	+2.74	+32.8	1.04f
Ceco Env	CECE	5.48	...	3.31	6.30	+.04	+38.7	...
Cedar Fair	FUN	15.00	...	7.90	15.80	+.64	+31.5	0.25e
Chemed Corp	CHE	62.54	+.22	43.88	62.83	+1.47	+30.4	0.56
Cheviot Financial Cp	CHEV	9.24	+.39	7.00	9.55	-.16	+25.0	0.44
Chiquita Brands Intl	CQB	12.04	+.34	11.10	19.59	-.01	-33.3	...
Cincinnati Bell	CBB	2.52	+.02	2.27	3.74	+.08	-27.0	...

3. What is the company symbol for Cedar Fair?
_____

4. What is the company name for CQB?
_____

5. What is the closing price of Am Financial Gp?
_____

6. What is the difference in the high and low prices of Ashland Inc. for the past year?
_____

7. Which companies' weekly change decreased?
_____

8. Which company had the lowest closing price for the day?
_____

9. Which company has the highest YTD % change?
   _____

10. How many companies paid dividends? List them.
    _____
    _____

11. List the companies that had no change in yesterday and today's closing prices.
    _____

12. How many shares of AtriCure Inc could you have purchased at the daily closing price with $151?
    _____

F.Y.I.

Blue chip stocks are the most consistently profitable and the most expensive. These are stocks of successful, established companies. They get their name from the blue chips in poker, which are the most valuable.

You will need to do some research and investigate companies before buying their stock. Do not buy stocks blindly. Examine companies whose products and services you and your friends use. Study companies that have been around a long time and have a history of profits. There may be costs associated with buying stocks. Make sure you consider these in your plans to purchase. A financial advisor, a person who helps people make decisions about their financial plans, can help you understand how to make good decisions when buying stock or other investments.

If you have limited money to invest, you may not want to use that money to buy stock in just one company. No matter how good the company is, it can be bought out. It can be taken over by another company, go bankrupt, or not make the profits you would like. If all your money is in that one company, you could lose everything you have saved and invested with them. An important concept in building your financial plan is diversification. **Diversification** simply means spreading out your risk by having several investments. You may have heard the saying, "don't put all of your eggs in one basket." When making investments, do not put all your money in one investment. Put your money into a variety of opportunities.

Check Your Understanding

Why is it important to diversify your investments?
_____
_____
_____

Reasons to Invest in Stocks

Investors buy stocks for several reasons. They want their investment to grow in value over time. They may want a regular income from the stocks in the form of dividends. They may hope to increase the amount of stock they own through stock splits.

Growth

Why buy stock? One reason is **growth**—the increase in the value of the stock. Suppose you pay $50 for a share of stock today. Hopefully, over a period of years the value of that stock will go up. If so, you can sell it for more than the $50 you paid for it, maybe quite a bit more.

Remember "average rate of return" from Chapter 1? You want your average rate of return over the time you hold the stock to be higher than with savings accounts. This higher return is the key to the growth of your investments. The "Rule of 72" applies to stock returns as well as savings. Divide 72 by your rate of return to figure out how many years it will take to double your investment.

Example 9-1

Your average rate of return is 3%. How many years will it take to double your investment?

Start with	72
Average rate of return	÷ 3
Number of years to double	24 years

You Do the Math 9-1

If your average rate of return is 8%. How many years will it take to double your investment?

Start with	_____
Average rate of return	_____
Number of years to double	_____

Example 9-2

You purchase 30 shares of stock in XYZ Company for $27.60 each. Your stock's rate of return varies each year over the 10 years that you keep the stock, as shown in the table below. How much profit will you earn if you sell after 10 years? What is the average rate of return?

Number of Shares x Price per Share = Total Amount of Purchase

Step 1 Calculate the purchase price of the stock

Price per share	$27.60
Number of shares	x 30
Total price of stock purchase	$828.00

Step 2 Calculate yearly earnings

Year	Beginning Balance	Rate of Return	Amount of Return	Ending Balance
1	$828.00	6.00%	$49.68	$877.68
2	877.68	5.00%	43.88	921.56
3	921.56	5.50%	50.69	972.25
4	972.25	8.00%	77.78	1,050.03
5	1,050.03	9.00%	94.50	1,144.53
6	1,144.53	7.25%	82.98	1,227.51
7	1,227.51	5.00%	61.38	1,288.89
8	1,288.89	2.50%	32.22	1,321.11
9	1,321.11	4.00%	52.84	1,373.95
10	1,373.95	3.00%	41.22	1,415.17

Step 3 Calculate your total earnings

Ending balance	$1,415.17
Cost of original purchase	− 828.00
Total earnings	$587.17

Step 4 Calculate average rate of return

Total earnings	$587.17
Number of years	÷ 10
Average yearly earnings	$58.72
Original investment	÷ 828.00
Average rate of return	7.1%

(Total Amount Earned ÷ Number of Years ÷ Original Investment = Average Rate of Return)

You Do the Math 9-2

You purchase 55 shares of stock in ABC, Inc. for $32.75 each. Your stock's rate of return varies each year over the 12 years that you keep the stock, as shown in the table below. How much profit will you earn if you sell after 12 years? What is the average rate of return?

Step 1 Calculate the purchase price of the stock

Price per share _____

Number of shares _____

Total price of stock purchase _____

Step 2 Calculate the yearly earnings

Year	Beginning Balance	Rate of Return	Amount of Return	Ending Balance
1	$1,801.25	9.00%		
2		6.00%		
3		5.50%		
4		8.00%		
5		9.00%		
6		7.25%		
7		5.00%		
8		3.50%		
9		4.00%		
10		3.00%		
11		6.00%		
12		9.00%		

Step 3 Calculate total earnings

Ending balance _____

Cost of original purchase _____

Total earnings _____

Step 4 Calculate average rate of return

Total earnings _____

Number of years _____

Average yearly earnings _____

Original investment _____

Average rate of return _____

Track Stocks

1. Choose five stocks from familiar companies to track over a two-month period. List the stocks in the table below.

2. Locate the stock quotes in the financial section of a newspaper to obtain the selling price of the five stocks. You can also find stock quotes on the Internet. Assume you are buying 100 shares of each stock. Record the total cost of those shares in column two.

3. At the end of two months, check the prices again. Using these prices, record the total price of 100 shares in column three.

4. If you sold your 100 shares after two months, what would your gain or loss be on each stock? Write your total gain or loss for each company in column four.

Company Name/ Symbol	Purchase Price of 100 Shares	Sale Price of 100 Shares	Gain or Loss
Totals			

Dividends

Another important reason to buy stock is to receive dividends. As explained earlier, a dividend is a share of the company's profits received by stockholders. Dividends may be issued quarterly, semiannually, or annually. That's right—the company gives you part of the earnings just for being an owner of the company.

Number of Shares × Dividend per Share = Total Dividend

Example 9-3

Company A issues dividends semiannually on its profits. For the current year, each share of stock earned $.75 semiannually. If you own 1,200 shares of Company A, what are your total dividends for the year?

Step 1 Calculate semiannual dividend

Number of shares owned	1,200
Dividend per share	× .75
Semiannual dividend	$900.00

Step 2 Calculate annual dividends

Semiannual dividend	$900.00
Number of times paid	× 2
Annual dividend	$1,800.00

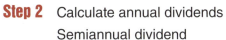 Do the Math 9-3

Company B issues quarterly dividends. For the current year, each share of stock earned $.35 each quarter. If you own 1,450 shares of Company B, what are your total dividends for the year?

Step 1 Calculate quarterly dividend

Number of shares owned	_____
Dividend per share	_____
Quarterly dividend	_____

Step 2 Calculate annual dividends

Quarterly dividend	_____
Number of times paid	_____
Annual dividend	_____

Stock Splits

Your stock may become more valuable through stock splits. A **stock split** is an increase in the number of shares without changing the total value of the shares. A stock split may occur when the price of a company's stock reaches a high price. The company may want to keep prices low enough for individuals to purchase the stock. A stock split lowers the price of the stock, but you now own more shares. For example, suppose you own 25 shares of a stock. If the company splits shares two for one, you now own 50 shares. In other words, you own more shares than you originally purchased without having to buy more. After the split, your individual shares will be worth less per share. Hopefully, the price will go up and you will profit from the stock split. Stock splits are usually a sign that the company is growing.

Example 9-4

You purchase 100 shares of Z Company stock at $36 per share. The company is doing well and decides to have a two-for-one stock split. How many shares will you have, and how much are they worth? Has the total value of your stock changed?

Step 1 Calculate the original value

Price per share	$36.00
Number of shares purchased	× 100
Original value of 100 shares	$3,600.00

Step 2 Calculate the value after stock split

Price per share	$18.00
Number of shares owned	× 200
Total value of shares	$3,600.00

Has the total value changed? No

You Do the Math 9-4

You purchase 175 shares of Beta Company stock at $52 per share. The company decides to have a two-for-one stock split. How many shares will you now have, and how much are they worth? Has the total value of your stock changed?

Step 1 Calculate the original value

Price per share _____

Number of shares purchased _____

Original value of 175 shares _____

Step 2 Calculate the value after stock split

Price per share _____

Number of shares owned _____

Total value of shares _____

Has the total value changed? _____

Check Your Understanding

Explain why investors may buy stocks.

_____
_____
_____
_____

Being Financially Responsible

Looking for the Right Investment A Checklist

As a financially responsible person, you should always be looking at the status of your plan as you go through the different stages of your life. This is the time to start thinking about your investments. Use this checklist to help you as you think about your financial plan.

Yes	No	
____	____	1. Am I currently saving anything toward my short-term or long-term goals?
____	____	2. Will I have enough money to meet my long-term or short-term goals?
____	____	3. Do I have enough time to reach my financial goals?
____	____	4. Do I make enough each month from my job to meet my goals?
____	____	5. Could I reduce my expenses each month?
____	____	6. Am I willing to give up some things I now spend money for in order to have money for investing?
____	____	7. Do I currently have any investments?
____	____	8. If I do have investments, are they diversified?
____	____	9. Am I willing to take risks?
____	____	10. Do I have a mentor that will help me get started?

Do an Internet search for financial calculators. Find one that focuses on investments. Go through the various topics in the calculator. How can this information help you when deciding how to invest your money?

Mutual Funds

Because there is a risk in buying individual stocks, you may want to consider investing in mutual funds. **Mutual funds** are professionally managed investments. They offer diversification and liquidity. (They can be easily turned into cash.) A mutual fund uses the money of many individuals pooled together. The pooled money is invested in a group of stocks. Bonds are also included in some mutual funds.

Mutual funds spread out your risk. If one, two, or ten companies in your fund go bankrupt, you still have ownership of many other companies. There may be as many as 50 to 100 companies in one mutual fund. You can buy a share of the fund and own fractions of shares in all of the companies in the

F.Y.I.
If you are hesitant to buy stock in certain types of companies, you can avoid funds that hold stock in those kinds of businesses. These funds are sometimes called socially responsible funds.

fund with the same amount of money that may only allow you to purchase a few shares of a single company's stock. It is a great way for a young person to begin investing in the stock market with small amounts of money.

Mutual funds are managed by professionals who study the market. They know what is going on with the companies in the fund. They can make informed decisions about buying and selling shares in the fund. Some people feel more comfortable buying mutual funds to begin investing in the stock market than buying individual stocks.

Mutual funds may be purchased at investment companies, brokerage houses, and some banks. Some mutual funds require large amounts of money to get started. However, there are some that require as little as $250 to $500. Some will even allow you to open a savings account until you build up enough to buy into the mutual fund.

Figure 9-3 shows a comparison of investments for a period of 25 years. A single stock is compared to multiple stocks. The value of the stocks after 25 years will vary greatly depending on the average rate of return for each one. If you invest in only one stock and it does poorly, you could gain very little or even lose your original investment. When you invest in several different stocks, you may earn a good rate of return overall. This is true even if some stocks do poorly or become worthless. Mutual funds work in a similar way. Even when some stocks in the fund do poorly, the overall result may be good.

> **F.Y.I.**
> Mutual funds hold approximately 22% of all publicly traded U.S. stocks. Remember to do some research and find out what the costs are going to be before you invest.

Check Your Understanding

Explain the difference between mutual funds and individual stocks. Why may mutual funds be important in your investment plan?

_____
_____
_____
_____

Figure 9-3 Comparison of Investments

INVESTMENT COMPARISON OVER 25 YEARS			
Single Investments		Multiple Investments	
Amount Invested	Current Value	Amounts Invested	Current Value
$100,000 earns 8% avg. return	$684,848	$20,000 becomes worthless	$0
		$20,000 earns 0%	$20,000
		$20,000 earns 5% avg. return	$67,727
		$20,000 earns 10% avg. return	$216,694
		$20,000 earns 15% avg. return	$658,848
Total Value	$684,848		$963,221

Bonds

Bonds, unlike stocks, do not make you a part owner of a company. A **bond** is essentially a loan for a set period of time. It is a certificate of debt issued by a government or company. The buyer is paid interest on the money invested, typically once or twice a year. When the bond matures, usually in 10 to 20 years, you are paid back the amount you invested. The percentage of interest you earn is called the **coupon rate**. There are three major bond categories: corporate, municipal, and U.S. government bonds.

Corporate bonds are issued by a business to raise money for operating expenses or expansion. High-grade corporate bonds are usually safer investments than stocks. However, they may have lower earnings than stocks over the long run.

Example 9-5

You purchase 50 corporate bonds from Ace Manufacturing Co. at $250 each. You earn a 5% coupon rate annually on your bonds until they mature in 10 years. At that time, you will be repaid the amount you invested. How much will you earn over the 10 years? If your income tax rate is 25%, what are your net earnings on the bonds?

Step 1 Calculate total amount of bonds

Amount per bond	$250.00
Number of bonds purchased	× 50
Total amount of bonds	$12,500.00

Step 2 Calculate interest

Total amount of bonds	$12,500.00
Coupon rate	× .05
Annual interest earned	$625.00
Number of years until maturity	× 10
Total interest earned	$6,250.00

Step 3 Calculate income tax

Interest earned	$6,250.00
Income tax rate	× .25
Income tax	$1,562.50

Step 4 Calculate net earnings

Interest earned	$6,250.00
Income tax	− 1,562.50
Net earnings	$4,687.50

You Do the Math 9-5

You purchase 60 corporate bonds from Perez, Inc. at $75 each. You will earn a 6.75% coupon rate on your bonds each year until they mature in 15 years. At that time, you will be repaid the amount you invested. How much will you earn over the 15 years? If your income tax rate is 28%, what are your net earnings on the bonds?

Step 1 Calculate total amount of bonds

Amount per bond _____

Number of bonds purchased _____

Total amount of bonds _____

Step 2 Calculate interest

Total amount of bonds _____

Coupon rate _____

Annual interest earned _____

Number of years until maturity _____

Total interest earned _____

Step 3 Calculate income tax

Interest earned _____

Income tax rate _____

Income tax _____

Step 4 Calculate net earnings

Interest earned _____

Income tax _____

Net earnings _____

Municipal bonds are issued by state, county, or city governments. Interest earned from municipal bonds is exempt from federal income tax. It may also be exempt from state and local tax. Parks and other recreational areas in your city or town may have been funded by municipal bonds.

Example 9-6

You purchase 75 municipal bonds issued by your city to build a swimming pool at a price of $175 each. You will earn a 5.5% coupon rate on your bonds each year for 20 years when they will mature. At that time, you will receive your loan repayment. How much will you earn on your bonds? You will not pay income tax on municipal bonds, so you do not have to figure tax.

Step 1 Calculate total amount of bonds

Amount per bond	$175.00
Number of bonds purchased	× 75
Total amount of bonds	$13,125.00

Step 2 Calculate interest

Total amount of bonds	$13,125.00
Coupon rate	× .055
Annual interest earned	$721.88
Number of years until maturity	× 20
Total interest earned	$14,437.60

You Do the Math 9-6

You purchase 85 municipal bonds issued by your county to build a skate park at a price of $125 each. You earn a 4.75% coupon rate on your bonds each year until they mature in 10 years and you receive your money back. How much will you earn on your bonds? Since no income tax is paid on municipal bonds, you do not need to calculate tax.

Step 1 Calculate total amount of bonds

Amount per bond	_____
Number of bonds purchased	_____
Total amount of bonds	_____

Step 2 Calculate interest

Total amount of bonds	_____
Coupon rate	_____
Annual interest earned	_____
Number of years until maturity	_____
Total interest earned	_____

U.S. savings bonds are the most common type of government bonds.

Shutterstock

U. S. savings bonds are issued by the U.S. Treasury Department. They are the safest bonds available since they are backed by the U.S. government. These bonds are issued in increments of $25 to $10,000. However, they do not pay a very high return and there is no secondary market for bonds. They cannot be bought and sold after they are purchased. Government bonds are exempt from state and local taxes, and federal taxes are only paid when the bond is redeemed. If the proceeds are used for tuition expenses, there is no federal tax due.

U.S. savings bonds are probably the most common type of government bonds. You may have one that you received as a gift at some point in your life. Savings bonds, known as series EE bonds, are bought at a bank or online. If you buy a paper series EE bond, you will pay half the face value. This means that you would pay $25 for a bond that at maturity will be worth $50. The Treasury Department guarantees that new issues of series EE savings bonds will double in value by 20 years from the issue date. If you buy a bond from the Treasury Department online, you will pay the face value. This means that if you pay $50 for the bond, it will be worth $50 plus interest when you cash it in at maturity.

There are other types of government bonds that are good short-term or long-term investments. You will want to talk to a financial advisor for more information when you are ready to make this type of investment.

 **Check Your Understanding**

List and describe the three types of bonds. How are they similar and how do they differ?

_____
_____
_____
_____
_____
_____
_____

Investing Now

In addition to stocks, mutual funds, and bonds, there are other ways to invest your money. You should research these options carefully before you decide whether they are right for you.

- Some people buy real estate as a long-term investment. Before investing in property, you should be educated on all the financial and legal aspects involved.
- Collectibles, such as sports memorabilia and stamp collections, sometimes increase in value. An expert opinion is needed to determine if these are good choices.
- Metals, such as gold and silver, can sometimes be a good investment.
- Gemstones, such as diamonds and emeralds, may also be an option for investments.

There are laws that protect the consumer from lender and seller abuse. If you have any questions about investments, seek advice from a professional to learn about the laws that protect you as a consumer.

 **Check Your Understanding**

What are some types of investments you might consider other than stocks, mutual funds, and bonds?

_____
_____

Investment Portfolio

1. Many people have a variety of investments that make up their portfolio. What investments do you have? Complete the following chart with assets you own that are considered investments.

Type of Investment	Name/Company	Value
Stocks		
Bonds		
Mutual Funds		
Collectibles		
Jewelry		
Precious Metals or Coins		
Musical Instruments		
Other		

2. What are some investments you might accumulate as you get older?

_____
_____
_____
_____

The securities and other assets you own make up your **investment portfolio**. Many experts suggest that when you are young, you should own more stocks than bonds. However, the most important thing to remember when investing is to diversify. Make sure you include a variety of investments. Remember that you can make changes in your portfolio as you get older.

A great way to begin investing is to set aside a specific amount of money each month to put into your investments. **Dollar-cost averaging** is investing a fixed dollar amount at regular intervals, usually monthly, without regard to the price at the time. When buying stocks, for example, if prices are high, you get fewer shares. However, when prices are low, you get more shares. Dollar-cost averaging is a disciplined approach to investing. It prevents you from investing a large lump sum when it may not be the best time to buy.

The ideal time to begin investing is when you are working part-time and living with your family without many expenses of your own. You can start a custodial brokerage account with a parent or guardian before you are 18. When you turn 18, you will no longer need your custodian's name on the account.

Suppose you are working part-time at your local mall or fast-food restaurant earning about $400 per month. You decide you do not want to work in a restaurant for the rest of your life. (You would rather own a portion of the company.) You decide to invest in a mutual fund that includes your store or restaurant in its fifty companies. You begin saving $100 per month as part of your financial plan. You're on your way to building your portfolio.

When you get a full-time job, adjust your contributions accordingly. In addition, always set aside more for investing each time you get a raise in salary. A good rule of thumb is to save a minimum of ten percent of your salary. However, if you cannot start there, then begin with 3% or 5% and work your way up. It is better to set a percentage rather than a dollar amount. That way when you get a raise, you will be saving more as well as having more to spend.

How will you have the discipline to save money each month? One way is to have your paycheck directly deposited to your bank account. Have the bank transfer part of it to a savings or investment account. If direct deposit (see Chapter 2) for your paycheck is not available, get in the habit of putting 10% in your bank account when you cash your check. This way, you will be less likely to spend it. You will not miss it, because you never get your hands on it.

Regular investing is important as well as the amount of the investments. Get in the habit of investing at an early age. Pay yourself first—in other words, do not promise yourself you will invest what you have "left over" at the end of the month. It won't happen! Include money for investing in your monthly budget. Paying yourself first is an excellent life-long habit to establish while young.

Check Your Understanding

Explain how you can begin investing now with limited funds.

_____
_____
_____
_____
_____
_____
_____

Saving for Investments

Keep track of every cent you spend for two weeks. You may be amazed at how much money you spend. How many snacks do you consume daily? How many DVDs, video games, or music downloads have you purchased in the last month? Remember to record every penny spent.

Day	Amount Spent	Items Purchased
Monday		
Tuesday		
Wednesday		
Thursday		
Friday		
Saturday		
Sunday		
Monday		
Tuesday		
Wednesday		
Thursday		
Friday		
Saturday		
Sunday		

1. How much did you spend in two weeks?

2. How much of this amount could you have saved and put toward an investment?

Dollars and $ense

Your First Investment

Making investments is sometimes easier said than done. If you do not have a job, you may think you cannot start a portfolio and make an investment. However, the truth is, even if you have $100 you can make an investment and start a portfolio. How can you do that? There are several investments you can make to get started.

- Savings Bonds. Perhaps someone has given you a series EE U.S. savings bond as a gift at some point in your life. The interest rate on these compounds semi-annually for 30 years. However, you can cash them before the full 30 years passes. Go to www.treasurydirect.gov to find out more information about savings bonds you may have or to find information about purchasing a bond.
- Treasury Bonds. Treasury bonds are interest-bearing bonds that pay semiannual interest. Maturity and interest rates may fluctuate. Go to www.treasurydirect.gov to find out more information about treasury bonds.
- Stocks. Technically, there is no minimum number of shares you must purchase from a publicly traded company. Before you buy, however, you need advice from a broker or financial advisor who can help you set up a plan to buy stocks on a schedule.
- Mutual Funds. Mutual funds are a great way to create retirement funds or educational funds. Many banks sell mutual funds. They will explain the programs to help you to make decisions about your investment. You can also ask a reliable financial advisor for help to get started.

Think big, start small. Before you know it, you will be on your way to creating an investment portfolio that will get you started on a solid financial plan.

Chapter Review

Summary

Investing is buying securities or other assets in an effort to increase your wealth over time. The most common types of securities are stocks and bonds. There are two basic types of stock—common and preferred. Investors buy stocks for several reasons. They want their investment to grow over time through rising stock prices or stock splits. They may also want a regular income in the form of dividends.

A mutual fund uses the money of many individuals pooled together to buy stocks and bonds. These professionally managed investments provide a simple way to diversify your holdings.

A bond is a certificate of debt issued by a government or company. The buyer is paid interest on the money invested. There are three major bond categories: corporate, municipal, and U.S. government bonds. In addition to securities, there are other ways to invest your money. Real estate, collectibles, and precious metal are examples of other investment options. Regular investing is important as well as the amount of the investments. You should get in the habit of investing at an early age. Pay yourself first by including money for investments in your monthly budget.

Review Your Knowledge

Circle the correct answer for each of the following.

1. The amount of money you invest is called
   A. growth.
   B. principal.
   C. coupon rate.
   D. dividends.
2. A piece of the ownership of a company is called a(n)
   A. principal.
   B. dividend.
   C. stock.
   D. bond.

3. A corporation that does not sell its stock to the general public is called a(n)
   A. partnership.
   B. public company.
   C. privately held company.
   D. None of the above.
4. Ups and downs in the stock market are known as
   A. fluctuations.
   B. investments.
   C. recessions.
   D. expansions.
5. Upward trends in the stock market are called
   A. fluctuations.
   B. investments.
   C. recessions.
   D. expansions.
6. When companies share profits with stockholders, this is called
   A. dividends.
   B. growth.
   C. a stock split.
   D. a blue chip stock.
7. Spreading out risk in your investments is called
   A. fluctuation.
   B. investment.
   C. dollar-cost averaging.
   D. diversification.
8. If you lend money to a company in exchange for receiving interest, you are buying
   A. stocks.
   B. bonds.
   C. real estate.
   D. portfolios.
9. Bonds sold by cities or towns are called
   A. U.S. savings bonds.
   B. municipal bonds.
   C. corporate bonds.
   D. coupon bonds.
10. Regularly buying investments with a set amount of money each month without regard to the price at the time is called
    A. buying common stock.
    B. buying bonds.
    C. diversification.
    D. dollar-cost averaging.

Build Your Vocabulary

For each word or term, write the correct definition using your own words.

11. Investing

12. Security

13. Common stock

14. Preferred stock

15. Recession

16. Bull market

17. Bear market

18. Stock split

19. Mutual funds

20. Investment portfolio

_____

_____

Apply Your Math Skills

Calculate the answers to the following problems.

21. If your average rate of return is 9%, how many years will it take you to double your investment?

_____

22. You purchase 50 shares of stock in GWP, Inc. for $38.90 each. Your stock's rate of return varies each year over the five years that you keep the stock, as shown in the table below. How much profit will you earn if you sell after five years? What is the average rate of return? Show all of your work below.

Step 1 Calculate purchase price of the stock

Price per share _____

Number of shares _____

Total price of stock purchase _____

Step 2 Calculate yearly earnings

Year	Beginning Balance	Rate of Return	Amount of Return	Ending Balance
1	$1,945.00	6.00%		
2	2,061.70	5.00%		
3	2,164.79	4.50%		
4	2,262.20	5.00%		
5	2,375.31	5.50%		

Step 3 Calculate total earnings

Ending balance _____

Cost of original purchase _____

Total earnings _____

Step 4 Calculate average rate of return

Total earnings _____

Number of years _____

Average yearly earnings _____

Original investment _____

Average rate of return _____

23. Company Y issues dividends quarterly. For the current year, each share of stock earned $.35 each quarter. What are your total dividends for the year if you own 375 shares of Company Y? Show all of your work below.

24. You purchase 165 shares of Alpha Company stock at $49.50 per share. The company decides to have a two-for-one stock split. How many shares will you have after the split and how much are they worth? Has the total value of your stock changed?

_____
_____
_____

25. You purchase 45 corporate bonds from Baltic Manufacturing at $235 each. You will earn 4.35% interest on your bonds each year until they mature in 10 years. At that time, you will be repaid the amount you invested. How much will you earn over the 10 years? If your income tax rate is 25%, what are your net earnings on the bonds? Show all of your work below.

26. You purchase 25 municipal bonds issued by your county to build a park at $145 each. You will earn 4.9% interest on your bonds each year for 15 years. At that time, you will receive your loan repayment. How much will you earn on your bonds? Remember, you will not pay income tax on municipal bonds. Show all of your work below.

10 Retirement Planning: Looking Toward the Future

Terms

Social Security
Supplement
Retirement account
Tax deferred
Contribution
Distribution
IRA
Earned income

Roth IRA
401(k)
Rollover
403(b)

Objectives

When you complete Chapter 10, you will be able to:

- **Explain** the importance of planning for retirement.
- **Describe** Social Security and the role it plays for retirees.
- **Discuss** the various retirement accounts that are available to most workers.

Chapter 10 Retirement Planning: Looking Toward the Future

Before you read this chapter, answer the following questions to see how much you already know about retirement planning.

1. What is retirement?

2. What does it mean to plan for retirement?

3. At what age should you start thinking about retirement?

4. At what age will you be able to retire?

5. Where does money come from to live on after you have retired?

6. How much money do you think you will need to live on when you retire?

7. What Social Security benefits are available for people who are retired?

8. What is an IRA?

9. What is a 401(k)?

10. What is a Roth IRA?

Retirement Planning

Retirement is probably the last thing on your mind right now, but now is exactly the time to start saving for it. By starting in your late teens or early adult years, you can save for retirement without having to give up half your paycheck. Remember, time is important when planning for retirement—and you have lots of time!

In years past, many people thought they would need less money in their retirement years than they did while they were working. To some extent, that idea makes sense. For example, you may no longer be paying for a mortgage on a home during retirement. Your children's college expenses may be paid. You may have lower costs for other things, such as clothing and cars, than when you were working.

However, many people want to keep or even increase their level of income as they get older so they can keep the same life style. Other expenses may take the place of working expenses. You may want to travel, purchase a vacation home, or save money for your grandchildren's education. Everyone wants the same thing—enough money to live comfortably.

Your retirement planning will involve many factors. For example, when you are ready to retire, you may decide it is time to sell some of your stocks and bonds. You may sell real estate or withdraw money from savings accounts. During retirement, you will need to balance your available income with expenses. The income may be from investments, Social Security, and retirement accounts. You should plan to have enough retirement savings to replace 80% of your annual working income.

The older generation of Americans is living longer and healthier. They are traveling and doing things they did not have time to do when they were younger—if they are financially secure. No matter what choices you make to start saving for retirement, the very best decision is to start now. Remember, time is on your side. You can start saving small amounts of money now rather than having to save large amounts if you wait.

F.Y.I. Studies suggest that more than 40% of Americans will not be able to maintain their current standard of living when they retire.

Check Your Understanding

Why should you think about retirement now instead of waiting until you are older?

_____

_____

_____

Social Security

When you retire, you may be able to collect Social Security benefits. As you learned in Chapter 2, **Social Security** is a social insurance program run by the U.S. government. It provides benefits for retired workers, the disabled, and other qualified persons. It is funded by taxes paid by workers and their employers. You begin paying into Social Security taxes when you begin working, even part-time, at most jobs. Your employer matches the amount of taxes you pay.

You may be able to retire at age 67. The amount you will receive will depend on how long you worked as well as how much you earned. If you become disabled, you may be able to collect benefits. If you should die, your family may be able to collect your Social Security benefits. Think of Social Security as a **supplement** (an extra amount) to what you have invested and saved for your retirement. Do not count on it as the main source of your retirement income. After you start working, you will receive a statement that shows how much you have paid into Social Security each year. The statement will have information similar to that shown in Figure 10-1.

Figure 10-1 Statement of Earnings

Your Earnings Record		
Years You Worked	Your Taxed Social Security Earnings	Your Taxed Medicare Earnings
2008	$580	$580
2009	1,380	1,380
2010	2,455	2,455

Along with this information, you will get an estimate of how much you will be able to collect when you retire. Part of a sample estimate is shown in Figure 10-2. Over the course of your working years, this yearly statement from Social Security will help you plan for your retirement. However, keep in mind that this data can change. There is little doubt that changes will be made to the Social Security system in coming years. Remember, do not count on Social Security for enough money to live on during retirement. Consider it as a supplement to your other retirement income.

Figure 10-2 Sample Benefits Statements

Your Estimated Benefits		
Retirement	You have earned enough credits to qualify for benefits. At your current earnings rate, if you continue working until…	
	your full retirement age (67 years), your payment would be about…	$1,478 a month
	age 70, your payment would be about…	$1,867 a month
	age 62, your payment would be about…	$1,088 a month

Example 10-1

You are 16 years old and earn the youth minimum wage of $4.25 per hour at your summer job. You work a total of 300 hours. Your employer withholds 6.2% of your earnings for Social Security. What are your total earnings? How much will your employer withhold for your Social Security taxes? How much will your employer pay for you? What is the total amount paid into your account?

Step 1 Calculate total earnings

Hourly rate	$4.25
Total hours worked	× 300
Total earnings	$1,275.00

Step 2 Calculate total amount

Total earnings	$1,275.00
Social Security tax rate	× .062
Amount withheld from employee	$79.05
Employer's equal contribution	+ 79.05
Total amount	$158.10

You Do the Math 10-1

You are 20 years old and earn the minimum wage of $7.25 per hour. You work part-time while attending college. This year you worked 1,200 hours. What are your total earnings? How much will your employer withhold for your Social Security taxes? How much will your employer pay for you? What is the total amount paid into your account?

Step 1 Calculate total earnings

Hourly rate	_____
Total hours worked	_____
Total earnings	_____

Step 2 Calculate total amount

Total earnings	_____
Social Security tax rate	_____
Amount withheld from employee	_____
Employer's equal contribution	_____
Total amount	_____

Check Your Understanding

Describe Social Security and the role it plays for retirees.

_____
_____
_____
_____
_____
_____
_____

Social Security Benefits

Go to Social Security Online at www.ssa.gov to learn about retirement benefits. Select the Retirement link. Read the information you find and answer the following questions.

1. You have to become eligible for Social Security benefits by working. You are given "credits" each year you work. What are credits based on? (Search the site using the term *credits* to find information.)

   _____

2. The retirement age changes depending on the year you were born. What year can you retire and receive full Social Security benefits? How old will you be?

   _____
   _____

3. How much will your Social Security check be reduced if you retire early at age 62?

   _____
   _____

4. Will your benefits be taxable?

___

Retirement Accounts

Americans are being asked to plan for their retirement and not to depend too heavily on Social Security. However, many people are still not saving nearly enough.

Part of your financial planning should include retirement accounts. A **retirement account** is an investment set up to provide income in your later years. During that time, you may not be able or may not want to work.

Many retirement accounts are **tax deferred**. This means you do not pay taxes now on the money you put in the account. The money you put into this account is called a **contribution**. The earnings from your retirement account are not taxed when earned. However, you will pay tax on the money you withdraw from a tax-deferred account. This money is called a **distribution**. Deferred means *delayed*—you are delaying the time when you will pay taxes on the money in tax-deferred accounts.

Example 10-2

You earn $32,000 and contribute $3,000 to a tax-deferred retirement account. How much of your income will be taxed? Your tax bracket is the rate you pay as a percent of your income. If you are in a 15% tax bracket, how much will you save in taxes?

Step 1 Calculate taxable income

Total earnings	$32,000.00
Tax-deferred retirement amount	− 3,000.00
Taxable earnings	$29,000.00

Step 2 Calculate tax savings

Income not taxed	$3,000.00
Tax rate	× .15
Amount of tax savings	$450.00

You Do the Math 10-2

Your annual earnings are $48,000. You contribute $5,000 this year to a tax-deferred retirement account. How much of your income will be taxed? If you are in a 25% tax bracket, how much will you save in taxes?

Step 1 Calculate taxable income

    Total earnings   _____

    Tax-deferred retirement amount   _____

    Taxable earnings   _____

Step 2 Calculate tax savings

    Income not taxed   _____

    Tax rate   _____

    Amount of tax savings   _____

Check Your Understanding

Explain how a retirement account can work for you.

_____

_____

There are several retirement account choices available. Four popular types are traditional IRAs, Roth IRAs, 401(k) plans, and 403(b) plans. Some accounts have limits on the amount you can contribute. Some are available only to people in certain types of jobs.

IRAs

IRA stands for *individual retirement account*. An IRA is a personal savings plan that gives you tax advantages for setting aside money for retirement. A traditional IRA may be part of your financial plan. IRAs are private accounts that you set up for contributing retirement money. There is no contribution from your employer. You can open an IRA if you have taxable compensation and are younger than age 70 1/2. Taxable compensation is sometimes called earned income. **Earned income** is money you receive from wages, salaries, commissions, and a few other types of income. There are limits and other rules that affect the amount that you can contribute to an IRA each year. Always check the tax laws to find current limits. Limits also apply if your employer offers a retirement plan, so do some research.

When you set up an IRA, you deduct the amount you contribute from your current taxable income. You pay tax later when you take money out

F.Y.I.
Parents and grandparents cannot start IRAs for young children because the children do not have earned income.

during your retirement. You can take money out of a traditional IRA at any time. However, you should plan not to withdraw money before you are at least 59 1/2 (with some exceptions). If you do withdraw money early, you may have to pay a 10% penalty in addition to the regular income taxes on the money. You must begin taking out money after you reach age 70 1/2.

Example 10-3

You need $5,000 for an emergency and decide to withdraw it from your traditional IRA retirement account before you are age 59 1/2. You are in a 25% tax bracket. How much will you actually receive as a net amount?

Step 1 Calculate 10% penalty

Amount withdrawn	$5,000.00
Penalty rate	× .10
Amount of penalty	$500.00

Step 2 Calculate tax paid

Amount withdrawn	$5,000.00
Tax rate	× .25
Amount of tax owed	$1,250.00

Step 3 Calculate total deductions

Penalty	$500.00
Tax	+ 1,250.00
Total amount of reduction	$1,750.00

Step 4 Calculate net amount received

Amount withdrawn	$5,000.00
Deductions	− 1,750.00
Amount received	$3,250.00

In reality, you would have to withdraw much more than the $5,000 you actually need from your account. Look at other options before you withdraw money from any retirement account.

You Do the Math 10-3

You decide to withdraw $7,500 from your traditional IRA for a down payment on a new car before you reach age 59 1/2. If you are in a 28% tax bracket, how much will you actually receive as a net amount?

Step 1 Calculate 10% penalty

Amount withdrawn	_____
Penalty rate	_____
Amount of penalty	_____

Step 2 Calculate tax paid

    Amount withdrawn   _____

    Tax rate   _____

    Amount of tax owed   _____

Step 3 Calculate total deductions

    Penalty

    Tax   _____

    Total amount of reduction   _____

Step 4 Calculate net amount received

    Amount withdrawn   _____

    Deductions   _____

    Amount received   _____

Check Your Understanding

What is a traditional IRA?

_____

_____

Withdrawing Money from an IRA

If you withdraw money early from a traditional IRA, you may have to pay a 10% penalty in addition to the regular income taxes on the money. If you are in a 28% tax bracket, this means that you will actually get only 62% of the money you withdraw. The other 38% will go to taxes and penalty.

You decide to take an early withdrawal from your IRA to cover an emergency expense. You need $5,000. How much money do you need to withdraw from the IRA to receive $5,000 after paying the penalty and taxes? (Hint: Divide the amount of money you want to receive by the percentage of the total you will receive.)

_____

_____

A Roth IRA is a good way to begin saving when you are in high school.

Roth IRA

A **Roth IRA** is an individual retirement account that does not have tax-deferred contributions. It is subject to many of the same rules as a traditional IRA. For example, to open a Roth IRA, you must have taxable compensation. Unlike a traditional IRA, amounts that you put in the account are not tax deductible. However, if you meet certain requirements, the money you draw out at retirement will be tax-free. This means that the earnings on the Roth IRA will be tax-free. The earnings might be from interest, for example, or an increase in the value of stocks in your Roth IRA.

You can open a Roth IRA if you are under age 18 with a parent or guardian on the account. Then when you turn 18, you can remove the guardian's name from the account. This is a good way to begin saving while you are in school working part-time. Chances are you are not paying tax on most, or any, of the amount you earn while in high school. Then, when you get a full-time career job after high school or college, you may be able to add a retirement account as a benefit from the company where you work. You can have both types of accounts if you meet certain requirements.

To be able to put money in a Roth IRA, your income must be less than certain amounts. The amounts vary and are related to the way you file taxes (single, married, etc.) and other factors. There are also limits on the amount you can contribute each year. The amount cannot be more than you have earned in that year. It also cannot be more than the maximum amount set by the government. Currently, the government permits a contribution of no more

---

F.Y.I.

One family encouraged their 16-year-old son to save $1,000 annually from part-time earnings. They matched that amount each year for three years. Upon graduation from high school, he had $6,000 in a Roth IRA. If the money remains in the account with an average rate of return of 10%, he will have over half a million dollars at age 65, with only $6,000 invested!

than $6,000 per year to a Roth IRA. This amount is $5,000 for people under age 50. There are some exceptions to these limits. You can find more information about income and contribution limits on the IRS website.

Qualified distributions from a Roth IRA are tax-free. On other distributions, you may have to pay a 10% tax penalty on the money you withdraw before age 59 1/2. Because the money you contribute to a Roth IRA has already been taxed, you may withdraw the *principal* at any age without paying a penalty or taxes. You may not withdraw the *earnings* without incurring a penalty until age 59 1/2. There are no required distributions from a Roth IRA starting at age 70 1/2.

Example 10-4

Your grandparents want to help you start a Roth IRA by giving you 50% of the total contribution. Your total earnings are $5,200 for your part-time job in high school. You want to contribute the maximum amount, $5,000. How much will you contribute? How much will your grandparents contribute?

Step 1 Calculate your contribution

Maximum contribution allowed	$5,000.00
Your contribution percentage	× .50
Amount of your contribution	$2,500.00

Step 2 Calculate grandparents' contribution

Maximum contribution allowed	$5,000.00
Grandparents' contribution percentage	× .50
Amount of grandparents' contribution	$2,500.00

Step 3 Calculate total amount contributed

Your contribution	$2,500.00
Grandparents' contribution	+ $2,500.00
Total amount of contribution	$5,000.00

You Do the Math 10-4

Your parents want to encourage you start a Roth IRA. They plan to give you 25% of the total contribution. Your total earnings are $4,750 for your part-time job in high school. You plan to open a Roth IRA with that amount. How much will you contribute? How much will your parents contribute?

Step 1 Calculate your contribution

Desired contribution	_____
Your contribution percentage	_____
Amount of your contribution	_____

Step 2 Calculate parents' contribution

Desired contribution _____

Parents' contribution percentage _____

Amount of parents' contribution _____

Step 3 Calculate total amount contributed

Your contribution _____

Parents' contribution _____

Total amount of contribution _____

Check Your Understanding

How do contributions to a Roth IRA differ from contributions to a traditional IRA?

_____

Web Connect

Roth IRAs

1. Research at least three investment companies that offer Roth IRAs by going to their websites. Record the company names in the table.

2. What is the minimum amount needed to open an IRA at each of these companies? What minimum amount (if any) must you contribute each month, quarter, or year? Enter the amounts in the table.

3. What fees are charged to open or maintain the account? Enter the amounts in the table.

Company	Minimum to Start	Monthly Amount	Annual Fees

Dollars and $ense

Starting a Roth IRA

You are a young person with plenty of time for saving and investing. Starting a Roth IRA is a very good first step. When you begin earning money, consider opening this kind of account as soon as possible.

Check with banks and investment companies for information on how to start an account.

Starting an account is as easy as filling out an application to open a checking account. You will need information such as the following:

- Two forms of identification
- Your Social Security number
- Name and contact information for your employer
- Names of your beneficiaries for the account
- The amount of your initial contribution to start the account

If you are under age 18, you will have to open an account with a parent or guardian. You may be able to open the account with as little as $100. However, you need to verify that with the investment company. Some investment companies will let you set up an automatic withdrawal from your bank account. This lets you invest regularly and helps you budget your money.

The investment counselor will give you information on the options you have to how to invest your money. In a Roth IRA, you may be able to diversify your dollars into mutual funds or other options that you select. Be sure to ask if there are any fees for the service. Before you open the account, do a search for *how to open a Roth IRA* on the Internet. Read articles so that you can be better prepared when you make the decision to open an account.

401(k)

As an employee benefit, many companies offer plans for employees to help them save for retirement. A **401(k)** is an employer-sponsored retirement plan. It allows you to put a part of your earnings into a tax-deferred investment plan.

Some employers match a portion of the amount that you contribute to a 401(k) plan. This is an excellent reason to start this type of retirement account. You may have to be a full-time employee to qualify. There is usually a limit that employers will match. For example, your employer might put in a dollar for every dollar you contribute to up to 5% of your gross salary. That's a direct 100% return on your money. It is hard to beat that kind of return! Take advantage of this opportunity and contribute at least the amount your employer will match each year.

There are limits to how much you can contribute each year to a 401(k). Do research to find the current limits. Contributions for a 401(k) are usually taken directly out of your paycheck. The money you contribute is deducted from your gross wages and reduces your taxable income. Most 401(k) withdrawals are taxable. You may also have to pay a 10% penalty if you are not age 59 1/2 or older when you take money out. There are some exceptions to this penalty rule.

> **F.Y.I.**
> *You may withdraw money any time from a retirement account. However, you jeopardize your retirement when you take money out early. You may also pay a heavy penalty.*

Be sure to maximize your contribution to your 401(k), especially if it is matched by your employer.

Shutterstock

You should have some options in selecting investments for your 401(k). Stay away from putting too large a portion into the company's own stock, especially if the matching funds are in company stock. Try not to have more than 10% of your 401(k) in your company's own stock. Remember to diversify when you invest.

Example 10-5

Last year you contributed 10% of your $37,500 salary to a 401(k) account. How much did you contribute? Your employer matched 100% of your contributions up to $3,000. What was the total contribution to the fund? Your investments in the fund had a 5.5% yearly average rate of return last year. How much did you have in earnings?

Step 1 Calculate your contribution

Your salary	$37,500.00
Contribution rate	× .10
Your 401(k) contribution	$3,750.00

Step 2 Calculate total contributions

Your contribution	$3,750.00
Employer's contribution	+ 3,000.00
Total 401(k) contribution	$6,750.00

Step 3 Calculate earnings

Total contributions to 401(k)	$6,750.00
Yearly average rate of return	× .055
Total earnings	$371.25

You Do the Math 10-5

Last year you contributed 8% of your $28,750 salary to a 401(k) account. How much did you contribute? Your employer matched 50% of your contributions, up to $5,000. What was the total contribution to the fund? Your investments in the fund had a 6.25% yearly average rate of return last year. How much did you have in earnings?

Step 1 Calculate your contribution

Your salary _____

Contribution rate _____

Your 401(k) contribution _____

Step 2 Calculate total contributions

Your contribution _____

Employer's contribution _____

Total 401(k) contribution _____

Step 3 Calculate earnings

Total contributions to 401(k) _____

Yearly average rate of return _____

Total earnings _____

The longer you stay at a company, the more you will benefit from your employer's contributions to your 401(k). If you leave the company, you may have the option to leave your 401(k) in the account to keep growing. You may also transfer it to a 401(k) provided by your next employer. Transferring your 401(k) to a new account is called a **rollover**. Make sure you have worked at your company long enough to take your 401(k) with you when you change jobs. There are strict regulations on rollovers from retirement accounts. Talk to a financial advisor to learn how to avoid paying penalties and taxes.

As with a traditional IRA, if you withdraw money from your 401(k) before age 59 1/2, you may have to pay a 10% penalty. This is in addition to paying income tax on the money. As with other types of accounts, there are some exceptions to this rule. After age 59 1/2, there is no penalty. However, you will have to pay income tax on the money.

F.Y.I. Many people who could open a 401(k) or other retirement accounts do not do so. Even when employers offer matching funds, they do not participate.

Check Your Understanding

Describe a 401(k) account and how it works as a retirement savings program.

_____
_____
_____
_____

Retirement for Teens

1. Do an Internet search for *retirement for teens*. Find and read at least two articles about retirement planning for teens.
2. For each article, write a paragraph or bulleted list that summarizes the information.
3. Give the article name and complete source information for each article.

_____
_____
_____
_____
_____

403(b)

A **403(b)** is a tax-deferred retirement plan. It is similar to a 401(k) plan. However, it is designed for public school teachers and employees of certain nonprofit organizations. Some employers match contributions by employees up to a certain amount.

Some 403(b) plans are set up and run by the employer. Other plans are run by a third party. Either way, your contributions to a 403(b) plan are typically deducted from your paycheck. As with other accounts, you usually have some options regarding how the money will be invested.

There are limits on the amount you may contribute each year and other rules. You are required to begin withdrawing money at age 70 1/2. You will have to pay tax on the amount of your withdrawals. If you withdraw funds before age 59 1/2, you will pay a 10% penalty plus the tax you owe on the amount withdrawn. There are some exceptions to this rule. You can learn about rules for a 403(b) plan on the IRS website.

Who is eligible for a 403(b)?

_____

_____

Planning for Retirement

Many young people think that retirement is too far away to worry about now. However, as you learned in this chapter, it is never too early to start thinking about saving money for this phase in your life. Keep in mind, not all people retire at 65. Those who are financially savvy may retire at an early age. So start planning today!

Complete the following statements to help you consider your earnings and retirement needs. Do a search on the Internet for a retirement calculator to help you complete statement 8.

1. I was born in _____. Based on my birth year, I will be able to collect full Social Security benefits at age _____.
2. I hope to earn $_____ each year for at least five years when I begin my career.
3. I plan to invest or save _____% of my income each year.
4. In my lifetime, I plan to work approximately _____ number of years.
5. I estimate (desire) that my average yearly salary will be $_____.
6. If I work approximately _____ years, I should earn approximately $_____ in my lifetime. (Hint: number of working years × yearly average salary)
7. As soon as I get my first job, I will be able to set up a(n) _____ account that will be my first retirement account.
8. When I retire, I think I will need $_____ in savings and investments.
9. The average Social Security payment for workers my age at retirement will be approximately $_____.
10. I hope to have investments when I retire, such as,_____
    _____.

Chapter Review

Summary

Although you may not have thought about retirement, your late teens is a good time to start saving for it. During retirement, you will need to balance your available income with expenses. When you retire, you may be able to collect Social Security benefits. The amount you will receive will depend on how long you worked as well as how much you earned. You may be able to collect benefits before retirement age if you become disabled. You should think of Social Security as a supplement to your other retirement income.

A retirement account is an investment set up to provide income in your later years. For some retirement accounts, the contributions are tax deferred. This is the case for traditional IRAs, 401(k) plans, and 403(b) plans. For Roth IRAs, you contribute money on which you have already paid taxes. However, the earnings that increase the account are tax-free. So you do not pay taxes on amounts withdrawn during retirement. There are rules relating to who may have different types of accounts and when the money may be withdrawn without penalties. There are also limits on contributions. Talk with a financial advisor and do research to learn details before opening an account. Typically, you have some options as to how the money in a retirement account is invested. Remember that it is important to diversify.

Review Your Knowledge

Circle the correct answer for each of the following.

1. Social Security is
   A. a social insurance program.
   B. run by the U.S. government.
   C. designed to provide benefits for retired workers and the disabled.
   D. All the above.

2. The amount of your Social Security benefit will depend on
   A. how long you worked.
   B. how much you earned.
   C. the age at which you begin collecting benefits.
   D. All the above.

3. Amounts of money that you pay into a retirement account are called
   A. supplements.
   B. distributions.
   C. contributions.
   D. rollovers.
4. Amounts of money that you withdraw from a retirement account are called
   A. supplements.
   B. distributions.
   C. contributions.
   D. rollovers.
5. For a traditional IRA
   A. the money you contribute is tax deductible.
   B. you do not need earned income to open an account.
   C. there is no limit on the amount per year that you can contribute.
   D. the money you contribute is not tax deductible.
6. For a Roth IRA,
   A. the money you contribute is tax deductible.
   B. the earnings will be tax-free.
   C. you must withdraw money at 70 1/2.
   D. you must be age 21 to open an account.
7. A 401(k) account
   A. is an employer-sponsored retirement plan.
   B. can include contributions from your employer.
   C. has limits on how much you can contribute each year.
   D. All the above.
8. Transferring funds from a 401(k) account with one employer to a 401(k) account with a new employer is called a(n)
   A. rollover.
   B. distribution.
   C. supplement.
   D. appreciation.
9. Amounts you put in a 401(k) account are
   A. supplements.
   B. distributions.
   C. tax-free.
   D. tax deferred.
10. A 403(b) account
    A. is a tax-free retirement plan.
    B. can be opened by anyone.
    C. is designed for public school teachers and employees of certain nonprofit organizations.
    D. may not be run by a third party but only by an employer.

Build Your Vocabulary

For each word or term, write the correct definition using your own words.

11. Retirement account

    _____

    _____

12. IRA

    _____

    _____

13. Earned income

    _____

    _____

14. 401(k)

    _____

    _____

    _____

    _____

15. 403(b)

    _____

    _____

Apply Your Math Skills

Calculate the answers to the following problems.

16. Your earnings are $35,000. You contribute $4,250 during the year to a tax-deferred retirement account. How much of your income will be taxed? If you are in a 25% tax bracket, how much will you save in taxes?

17. You are 17 years old and earn the youth minimum wage of $4.25 per hour at your summer job. You work a total of 250 hours. Your employer withholds 6.2% of your earnings for Social Security. What are your total earnings? How much will your employer withhold for your Social Security taxes? How much will your employer pay for you? What is the total amount paid into your account?

18. You withdraw $8,700 from your traditional IRA before you reach the age 59 1/2. If you are in a 15% tax bracket, how much will you actually receive as a net amount?

19. Your aunt is willing to give you 10% of the amount that you contribute to a Roth IRA. Your total earnings are $6,375. You want to contribute $1,600 (about 25% of your earnings). How much will you contribute? How much will your aunt contribute?

20. Last year you contributed 9% of your $45,690 salary to a 401(k) account. How much did you contribute? Your employer matched 100% of your contributions up to $3,500. What was the total contribution to the fund? Your investments in the fund had a 4.45% yearly average rate of return last year. How much did you have in earnings?

11
Your Financial Future: You Make the Choice

Terms

Rental property
Entrepreneur
Franchise fee
Franchise
Financial independence
Fiscal responsibility
Charitable contribution
Tax deductible
Gift
Ethics
Socially responsible
Talent

Objectives

When you complete Chapter 11, you will be able to:

- **Identify** additional options for your investment portfolio.
- **Discuss** planning for your financial independence.
- **Recognize** the importance of charitable contributions.

Your Financial IQ

Before you read this chapter, answer the following questions to see how much you already know about being financially responsible.

1. If you own an apartment building and rent to others, the building is considered an investment. What is an investment?
   _____
   _____

2. What does it mean to be an *entrepreneur*?
   _____
   _____

3. Define the term *franchise*.
   _____
   _____

4. How do you gain financial independence?
   _____
   _____

5. What does it mean to be diversified in your investments?
   _____
   _____

6. Why is it important to start saving now?
   _____
   _____

7. Describe what it means to have fiscal responsibility.
   _____
   _____

8. Making charitable contributions is a noteworthy activity. What does it mean to make a charitable contribution?
   _____
   _____

9. Write a sentence that describes your talents.
   _____
   _____

10. Why should you volunteer your time to organizations?
    _____
    _____

Your Investment Portfolio

In this text, you have learned how to become *money smart* through financial planning. You have also learned about taking advantage of opportunities for gaining financial independence. Money does not make you a better person—it just gives you choices.

Remember that you need to diversify and start saving early. These are keys to building wealth. As you begin to think past college and getting a job, you will want to develop your investment portfolio. In an earlier chapter, you learned about securities and retirement accounts. There are several other investments that you may also want to consider.

Rental Property

Rental property is an investment you may want to add to your portfolio. **Rental property** is real estate that you own and rent or lease to someone to generate income. Rental property could be a house, apartment, or office space.

Being a property owner brings with it financial responsibility. As a property owner, you must purchase the property, pay taxes and insurance, and maintain the property. It is essential that you have the money for these needs. It is also helpful if you are physically able to take care of minor repairs and maintenance. If you cannot take care of the property yourself, you will have to hire someone to do this for you.

You should be aware that renters may or may not take good care of your property. Even if you charge a sizeable deposit, it may not cover the cost of major repairs. Normal "wear and tear" is to be expected. For example, you will probably have to paint and replace carpeting when tenants move out of the property.

How do you decide what to charge for rental property? As a property owner, you will want to charge enough to cover your expenses and make a profit. It will be necessary to do research and calculate all the expenses that are involved with owning property. You will want to decide how much income you expect to make each month as you decide how much rent to charge.

> **F.Y.I.**
> As a property owner, you will need building insurance. This insurance will cover the cost of replacing your building in case of fire or other damage. You will also need liability insurance. It will protect you if someone is hurt or injured while on your property.

Check Your Understanding

Why is rental property considered an investment?

_____

_____

You may decide to make rental property part of your financial plan. However, there are many factors to consider before deciding whether this is a good investment for you. Make sure you understand the risks and rewards of being a property owner. Remember, real estate is a long-term investment.

Example 11-1

You have an apartment that you want to rent. Your mortgage payment is $428.75 per month. In addition, you pay the water bill, which averages around $45 each month. The tenants pay the other utilities. This month you have to replace a broken faucet and repair a leak in the sink, which totals $146.25. Your monthly insurance is $22. How much will your monthly expenses be for the property? If these are typical expenses each month, how much will you have to charge for monthly rent if you want to make a $50 profit each month?

Step 1 Calculate your costs for month

Mortgage payment on property	$428.75
Monthly water bill	45.00
Repairs	146.25
Insurance	+ 22.00
Total expenses estimated per month	$642.00

Step 2 Calculate monthly rental

Total expenses	$642.00
Anticipate profit each month	+ 50.00
Monthly rent	$692.00

You Do the Math 11-1

You want to rent a house to three college students. Your monthly mortgage payment for the house is $538.35. This month, you have to repair the front steps at a cost of $113.40. Your monthly building and liability insurance is $62.85. How much will your monthly expenses be for the property? If these are typical expenses each month, how much will you have to charge for monthly rent if you want to make a $100 profit each month?

Step 1 Calculate your costs for month

Mortgage payment   _____

Repairs   _____

Insurance   _____

Total expenses estimated per month _____

Step 2 Calculate monthly rental

Total expenses   _____

Anticipate profit each month   _____

Monthly rent   _____

Rental Property

You want to expand your investment portfolio and buy an office building. The building has three spaces that you will rent to make money. Answer the following questions.

1. How long do you think you would have to keep the property to make a return on your investment?
   _____
   _____

2. What types of challenges do you think you would have when trying to find someone to rent the offices?
   _____
   _____

3. As a property owner, what types of issues do you think you might have with people renting your building?
   _____
   _____

4. What kinds of other issues do you think property owners face with maintaining property?
   _____
   _____

Owning Your Own Business

As you grow in your career, you may decide to invest and start a business of your own. An **entrepreneur** is a person who organizes and operates a business. Being your own boss may be a worthy goal. However, you should realize that an entrepreneur is responsible for *everything* in the business. You will likely work more than 40 hours a week, especially for the first few years.

Many entrepreneurs start businesses in their chosen career field. They may have already been working in that field for many years and know that business. To start a business, you have to be persistent, have financial backing, and do your homework. The risks can be large, as can be the rewards. Many new businesses fail within the first five years. Therefore, it is important to have a solid financial plan before making the investment.

Franchise owners may have a greater chance at success than other entrepreneurs. This is because of the familiarity of their products to the public. In addition, they receive training and other help from the parent company. However, franchises must pay the parent company a **franchise fee** for the right to use its name. Most franchises are expensive to open. They are strictly regulated by the parent company and operate under the laws of the Federal Trade Commission.

Some people choose to buy an existing business or a franchise. A **franchise** is an agreement that allows you to sell a company's product or services in a certain location or area. Many such businesses may be familiar to you. (Think fast foods and clothing stores.) The local business is under the control of a parent corporation.

Entrepreneurs

Think of someone you know who owns a business. This could be a friend of the family who owns a local business. It could be someone famous, such as Bill Gates, one of the founders of Microsoft. List below some of the traits of that entrepreneur. What do you think motivated this person to start a business? What makes this person successful?

Franchises

1. Go to the Federal Trade Commission website. Select a link or search for *consumer protection*. Select available links or do a search to find information on *buying a franchise*. What questions does the bureau recommend that you ask before you invest in a franchise?

2. Do an Internet search to find businesses that are franchises. List five businesses that sell franchises to investors.

Financial Independence

As you learned in Chapter 1, **financial independence** is having enough money for your basic needs and modest wants without having to work. To reach the point where you can live on your investments, start preparing now while you are young. Time is a powerful factor in building wealth.

Your financial goals will change as you become established in your career and make life choices. Your income will depend on decisions you make about your career, your education, and the skills you develop. The sooner you create a financial plan, the better your chances are of attaining your goals. It does not take a lot of money to achieve wealth. A little money and a lot of time work very well.

There is never a convenient time to save, so start saving now. The more you make, the more you will probably spend. Pay yourself first by treating saving and investing as one of your monthly expenses. Be on the lookout for investments that will help you build wealth. Retirement accounts, mutual funds, rental property, or business ownership may all be a part of your portfolio. The *investment pyramid* in Figure 11-1 shows investment options and risks.

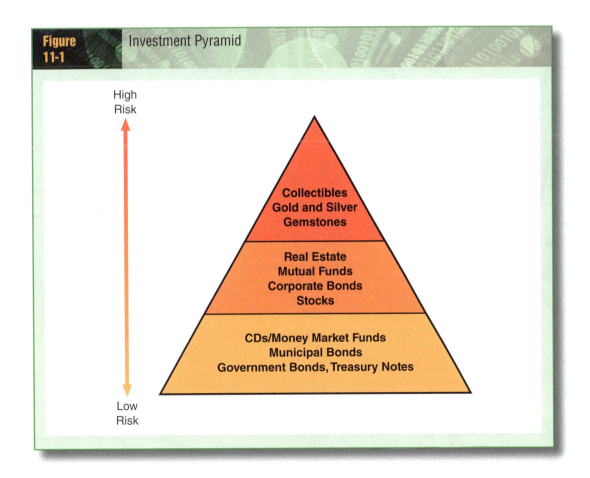

Figure 11-1 Investment Pyramid

Figure 11-2 shows a comparison of earnings when you begin investing at two different ages. Suppose you start saving $250 per month at age 25. You have a 7% rate of return compounded quarterly. You will have about $656,000 by age 65. If you wait until age 35 to start saving, you will need to save $500 per month (double the amount) to get close to the same results. You do not need to be reminded what the results will be if you wait until age 50!

It is important to develop fiscal responsibility. **Fiscal responsibility** is spending less than you make, or living below your means. Make sure you never borrow more money than you are able to repay and that you save enough to cover expenses for three to six months even if you lose your job. Look for opportunities to make the most of your current income. Begin now to achieve your own "financial independence day."

Figure 11-2 Benefits of Saving Early

Age 25	Age 35
$250 per month	$500 per month
7% rate of return	7% rate of return
40 years	30 years
$120,000 investment	$180,000 investment
= $656,339	= $612,173

Check Your Understanding

How can you begin planning for your financial independence now?

_____
_____
_____

Charitable Contributions

There is no doubt that being financially independent can provide more free time to enjoy life. If you start your nest egg at an early age, you will have the security of knowing that you can withstand financial setbacks. However, life is not about making money for the sake of being wealthy. In the long run, it is not how much you make, but what you do with your money and with your life that counts.

So now that you have become *money smart*, what do you do with your time and money as you work toward financial independence?

Making Contributions

A **charitable contribution** is a donation of money or gifts. For example, you might choose to give to a church, library, museum, or charity. Money you donate to a qualified charity is often **tax deductible**. The amount you give will reduce your taxable income. However, you may have to itemize when you file your tax return to take the deduction. You will also need to keep proof of your donation. When deciding how much to give, look at your income and expenses to see what you can afford to contribute. A donation of your time can be just as valuable to a charity as a monetary contribution.

Be responsible in your giving. Research organizations before you make a donation. This is especially a good idea if you are donating online. Make sure contributions go to the cause, not in the pockets of those who run the charity. Pay attention to the fine print that might say, "not all amounts are tax deductible." Many times only a portion of your contribution is tax deductible. If you buy tickets to a benefit dinner or concert, for example, only the portion above the normal cost of the ticket might be deductible.

> **F.Y.I.**
> Andrew Carnegie, for whom Carnegie Hall is named, said, "It is more difficult to give money away intelligently than earn it in the first place."

Example 11-2

You buy two tickets to a benefit dinner. The ticket price is $47.00 each. The dinner cost is $22.50 per person with the remainder going to a charity. How much is tax deductible?

Price of ticket	$47.00
Cost of dinner	− 22.50
Amount tax deductible per ticket	$24.50
Number of tickets purchased	× 2
Amount of tax deduction	$49.00

You Do the Math 11-2

You buy four tickets to a charity concert. The ticket price is $52.75 each. The concert would normally cost $27.95 per person. The proceeds will benefit a charity. How much is tax deductible?

Price of ticket	_____
Cost of concert	_____
Amount tax deductible per ticket	_____
Number of tickets purchased	_____
Amount of tax deduction	_____

In addition to money, you may also give gifts to charities. A **gift** is a voluntary transfer of assets. It is only considered a gift (or contribution) if no goods or services are expected in return. Many people donate stock, automobiles, and other assets to charities or religious organizations. The assets are valued at the current market value. If you plan to make a valuable contribution, get details first from the IRS website.

> **F.Y.I.**
> Used clothing, toys, or household goods can be donated to an organization such as Goodwill Industries. Donations help Goodwill fund job training and placement services. Buyers of the goods also benefit from low prices.

Charities

1. Visit the Better Business Bureau website and perform an Internet search for *charitable contributions*.

2. Select three charities to which you might consider contributing. Record their names in the table.

3. Research how much of each dollar goes to the actual charity recipients or activities and how much goes to administrative expenses. Record this information in the table.

Charity	Percent to Charity	Percent to Administration

Dollars and $ense

Citizenship

Life is not all about making money. Being a good citizen is important to your personal and financial success.

Good citizens are ethical. You probably hear the term ethics used almost every day, but do you know what the word means? **Ethics** are the principals that help you decide what is right and wrong. Being truthful, honest, and respecting others are important as you go through life, develop your career, and become a contributing citizen. Ethical behavior is expected when representing yourself and the business for which you work. Avoid the temptation to "twist the truth" and always keep your communication honest.

Good citizens are socially responsible. Being **socially responsible** means you have a concern for those around you. This concern extends not only to your community, but also to the country and the world. You show respect for others and lend a helping hand when possible. You also show concern for the environment.

Being ethical and socially responsible are important keys to your success.

Volunteering Your Time

While you are young, you may not have a lot of money for gifts and contributions. One thing you may be able to do is volunteer your time. There are many opportunities to volunteer your time. Community groups, animal shelters, elderly neighbors, churches, food pantries, and other organizations often need volunteers. Be aware that the value of the time you volunteer is not tax deductible.

Your school may require volunteer hours to meet graduation requirements. Make the most of those opportunities. Some may lead to a career later in life.

Do not discount your talents. **Talent** is a natural aptitude or ability to do something that comes easily to you. You may not be able to play the piano or guitar at a home for the elderly. However, you may be great at playing games with them one-on-one. Maybe you have a knack for making people feel welcome and comfortable. Perhaps you may want to stay behind the scenes and package food for a food pantry instead of serving it. You have a unique talent that some organization would be happy to use. Get out there and see what you can do!

Why do you think some schools require volunteer hours for graduation?

_____

_____

_____

_____

Your Talents

1. In the table below, list five of your talents that would benefit local charities.
2. How could your talents be put to use? Explain briefly in the second column of the table.

Talent	Organization and Activity

If you do not have enough money to provide a charitable donation to an organization, it is always beneficial to volunteer your time.

Money Smart

List the five most important things you have learned from this text that will help you become money smart.

1. _____
2. _____
3. _____
4. _____
5. _____

Financial Goals
A Checklist

Follow these simple steps to begin achieving your financial goals:

1. Get started! Start saving money today. Remember, time is on your side.
2. Create a financial plan early. Get in the habit of planning how you will spend and save your money.
3. Make the most of your earnings, no matter what the size of your paycheck. Make sure your paycheck is calculated correctly and that you understand all deductions.
4. Use budgets to control your spending and savings. Realize that budgets are a work in progress and will change frequently.
5. Shop around for banking services that best fit your needs. Develop a relationship with a bank so that you have a dependable resource for information.
6. Credit always ties up future income. Avoid using credit to buy what you do not need. Pay off credit cards in full each month. Know your credit score and how to keep it high. Practice discipline in using credit of any kind.
7. Protect yourself and your dependents with auto, health, and life insurance. Make sure you have renters insurance when renting an apartment or homeowners insurance when you buy a house. Research other insurance as you need it.
8. Ask questions and become money smart about financial matters. Take advantage of educational opportunities. Read books and financial pages of a newspaper. Talk to adults you trust about their challenges and successes with money.
9. Don't sign up for car loans for longer than four years. Try to make extra payments to pay the loan off early if you are able. Build equity in a home by paying down your mortgage. Never be underwater by owing more on an asset than it is worth.
10. Take advantage of investment opportunities and remember that diversifying and starting early are the keys to building wealth.
11. If you are currently working, open a Roth IRA now and a 401(k) when you get a full-time job.
12. Always consider taking advantage of good investment opportunities.
13. Give to charities and volunteer your time as your finances and schedule permit.
14. There are laws that protect the consumer from lender and seller abuse. If you have any questions about any financial decision you may be making, seek advice from a professional about the laws that protect you as a consumer.

Chapter Review

Summary

As you get older, there may be many opportunities for investing to become financially independent. Remember that you need to diversify and start saving early. You may choose to own rental property or own your own business. Buying a franchise may be a good way to open a business. Financial independence is having enough money for your basic needs and modest wants without having to work. To reach the point where you can live on your investments, start preparing now while you are young. Be financially responsible and be ethical in your dealings with others. You might choose to make gifts or contributions to a church, library, museum, or charity. Money you donate to a qualified charity is often tax deductible. You may also want to donate your time and use your talents to aid a charity or other organization.

Review Your Knowledge

Circle the correct answer for each of the following.

1. Property purchased with the idea of allowing persons to use it in return for payment is called
   A. a franchise.
   B. a gift.
   C. a contribution.
   D. rental real estate.

2. A person who owns a business is called a(n)
   A. entrepreneur.
   B. socially responsible person.
   C. contributor.
   D. renter.

3. An amount given to a charity is called a(n)
   A. entitlement.
   B. talent.
   C. contribution.
   D. franchise fee.

4. A gift is
   A. a voluntary transfer of assets with some goods or services expected in return.
   B. always tax deductible.
   C. never tax deductible.
   D. a voluntary transfer of assets with no goods or services expected in return.

5. Paying your bills on time is an example of
   A. timeshares.
   B. fiscal responsibility.
   C. franchise fees.
   D. entitlement.

6. Volunteering your time to a charity or other organization
   A. allows you to deduct the value of your time or work from your taxes.
   B. may help you meet graduation requirements.
   C. is probably not as valuable as giving money.
   D. All the above.

For each word or term, write the correct definition using your own words.

7. Franchise

8. Franchise fee

9. Ethics

10. Financial independence

11. Tax deductible

12. Talent

Apply Your Math Skills

Calculate the answers to the following problems.

13. You have an office space that you want to rent. Your mortgage payment is $367.50 per month. Insurance is $27.60 each month. This month you had to repair the air conditioning for $88.95 and a damaged door for $37.20. How much will your monthly expenses be for the property? If these are typical expenses each month, how much will you have to charge for monthly rent if you want to make a $150 profit each month?

14. You buy six tickets to a charity dinner. The ticket price is $36.45 each, but the cost of the dinner is $19.75 per person. The proceeds will benefit a charity. How much is tax deductible?

Glossary

401(k): An employer-sponsored retirement plan that allows you to put a part of your earnings into a tax-deferred investment plan.

403(b): A tax-deferred retirement plan similar to a 401(k) designed for public school teachers and employees of certain nonprofit organizations.

529 plan: A savings plan for education generally operated by a state or college; funds may be used for qualified colleges across the nation.

A

academic degree: An award given to a person by a college or other school signifying that the person has successfully completed a course of study.

adjustable rate mortgage (ARM): A secured loan with an interest rate that can change periodically.

allowances: Conditions for which you qualify that will lower the amount of income taxes withheld from your pay.

amortization: The process of making equal payments on a loan while reducing the principal.

annual percentage rate (APR): The interest rate on loans or credit cards that you are charged annually.

annual percentage yield (APY): Actual yield that is higher than the stated percentage rate because of compounding.

apartment lease: A contract outlining the conditions of an agreement to rent an apartment for a certain length of time, usually a year.

assessment: An amount required by the HOA to pay for major expenses.

assets: Things you own.

automatic teller machine (ATM): These allow you to withdraw cash from your account when your bank is closed or you are out of the area.

available credit: The difference between your credit card limit and the amount of credit you have already used.

277

average rate of return: The percentage that your savings or investments earn over a period of time.

B

bankruptcy: A legal decision that declares a person, company, or organization is unable to pay debts owed.

bear market: Occurs when stock prices are falling or staying at a low level.

beneficiary: A person or persons named in a life insurance policy to receive benefits.

benefits: Services or things of value that employees receive from employers in addition to their pay, such as vacation pay, group health insurance, and sick days.

bond: A loan to a company or government agency for a set period of time; buyer is paid interest and paid back his investment when the bond matures.

budget: An estimate, usually by category, of expected income and expenses for a given period of time.

bull market: Occurs when stock prices are rising.

C

capacity: Your ability to pay debts.

capital: The assets you have at your disposal.

car lease: A contract allowing the use of a vehicle in exchange for payment.

cash advance: A loan against the available credit on your credit card.

certificate of deposit (CD): An account earning a higher interest rate than a regular savings account; requires deposit for certain time periods and may require a minimum amount.

chapter 13 bankruptcy: Provides a payment plan to a trustee who pays creditors for you; stays on your credit report for seven years.

chapter 7 bankruptcy: A bankruptcy that eliminates most types of debt and stays on your credit report for 10 years; your property is sold to pay creditors.

charitable contribution: Money or gifts donated to a charity or other worthy cause.

check register: A record of checking account transactions showing deposits, payments, withdrawals, interest, and fees.

checking account: A type of bank account that allows you to make deposits, write checks, and withdraw your money at any time.

Consolidated Omnibus Budget Reconciliation Act (COBRA): Requires that you be allowed to continue health care provided through your employer after you have been laid off or have voluntarily left your job.

collateral: Property accepted as security for a debt, such as a car or home.

collision coverage: Insurance that pays for damage to your car from an accident.

common stock: Stock that earns dividends and has voting privileges on company policies and directors.

community college: A two-year school offering academic or occupational programs.

Glossary

compound interest: Earning interest on the principal plus the interest you have already earned.

comprehensive coverage: Insurance that pays for damage to your car unrelated to a collision.

contribution: The money you put into a retirement account.

corporate bonds: Bonds issued by businesses to raise money for operating expenses or expansion.

cosigner: Someone who agrees to pay your debt if you fail to pay.

coupon rate: Percentage of interest earned on a bond.

credit application: A form filled out to be considered for a loan that asks for credit history, job information, assets and other pertinent information.

credit bureau: An organization that keeps track of credit that is extended to you and the payments you make.

credit card: A plastic card that contains a name and account number allowing the holder to make purchases and pay for them at a later time.

credit history: The record of your prior credit purchases and payments.

credit report: A report listing credit cards, car loans, mortgages, and other type of credit extended to you; indicates payments, current balances, accounts you have opened or closed, and any late payments, claims from collection agencies, or defaults.

credit score: A number ranging from 500 to 850 that assembles all information in a credit report to indicate credit worthiness in one number; also called *FICO score*.

credit union: A nonprofit cooperative that exists to provide banking services to its members.

D

debit card: A card that allows users to withdraw money from a checking or savings account or to pay for purchases by having money drawn from the account.

deductible: The amount you will pay before your insurance company pays a claim.

deductions: The amounts subtracted from your gross pay.

default: The failure to pay a debt or other obligation.

depreciation: Decrease in the value of an asset.

direct deposit: A transfer of money (usually net pay) to a checking or savings account.

disability insurance: Insurance that pays a portion of your income if you are injured or ill and cannot work.

discretionary income: Money that remains after you have paid for regular or needed expenses.

distribution: The money withdrawn from a retirement account.

diversification: Spreading out your risk by having different investments.

dividend: A share of a company's profits received by stockholders.

dollar-cost averaging: Investing a fixed dollar amount at regular intervals, usually monthly, without regard to current price.

E

earned income: Money received from wages, salaries, commissions, and a few other types of income.

electronic banking: The transfer of funds by computer instead of using paper checks or cash, sometimes called *online banking*.

entrepreneur: A person who organizes and operates a business.

equity: The difference between what you owe on your house and its current market value.

escrow account: An account for holding money in trust for others.

estate: Your net worth; the value of your assets minus your debts.

estate planning: The process of arranging your financial affairs so that your wishes will be followed now and after your death.

ethics: The principles that help you decide what is right and wrong.

executor: A person who will carry out the wishes in your will and manage your estate.

expansion: The upward trends in the stock market.

expenses: Amounts paid for goods or services.

F

face value: The amount payable upon death; also called *death benefit*.

Federal Deposit Insurance Corporation (FDIC): An independent agency of the federal government that insures checking, savings, certificates of deposit, and money market accounts at most banks.

federal income taxes: Taxes on income collected by the U.S. government.

financial goals: Measurable objectives related to acquiring or spending money.

financial independence: Having enough money for your basic needs and modest wants without having to work.

financial plan: A set of goals or objectives for spending and saving your money.

fiscal responsibility: Spending less than you make, or living below your means; never borrowing more money than you are able to repay.

fixed expenses: Expenses that stay the same each month, such as school lunches or bus passes.

fixed rate mortgage: A secured loan with an interest rate that does not change.

fluctuations: The ups and downs in the stock market.

foreclosure: A process in which the lender takes possession of the house if you fail to make the mortgage payments.

franchise: An agreement that allows you to sell a company's product or services in a certain location or area.

franchise fee: A fee paid to the parent company for the right to use its name and sell its products.

G

gift: Voluntary transfer of assets.

grant: College funds usually provided by a nonprofit organization; grants are typically based on need and do not have to be repaid.

gross pay: The total amount of earnings before deductions.

growth: Increase in value of investments over a period of time.

H

health insurance: Protection against financial loss due to illnesses or injuries.

homeowners association (HOA) fees: Monthly or annual condo fees for insurance, upkeep of the buildings and common areas, landscaping, snow removal, and other amenities.

homeowners insurance: Insurance that covers a house and its contents.

I

income: Money you receive, such as pay from a job, gifts, or allowances.

individual retirement account (IRA): A personal savings plan giving you tax advantages for setting aside money for retirement.

installment loan: A purchase that is paid for in equal monthly payments.

insurance: Protection against financial loss that may occur in certain situations.

interest: Fees paid to borrow money or money earned on deposits with a bank or other financial institution.

intestate: The legal term for not having a will.

investing: Buying a financial product or asset in an effort to increase your wealth over time.

investment portfolio: The securities and other assets you own.

L

lessee: Person paying for the use of a vehicle or housing.

lessor: The property owner granting the lease of a vehicle or housing.

liabilities: Debts you owe

liability coverage: Insurance that protects those you may injure or whose property you may damage.

life insurance: Insurance that provides benefits after your death to persons you have selected.

lifelong learning: Acquiring new skills and knowledge throughout your lifetime for your career, for general knowledge in daily living, or for your personal interests.

liquid: An investment that can be bought, sold, or converted to cash quickly.

local income taxes: Taxes paid to a local government, such as a county or city, used for police departments, schools, county or city roads, and other local services.

M

Medicare: A national health insurance program run by the U.S. government.

mentor: Someone who shares knowledge and skills with you, usually on an informal basis.

money market account: Checking accounts that pay interest on the amount deposited in the account; usually require a minimum balance.

mortgage: A type of secured loan used for buying property.

municipal bonds: Bonds issued by state, county, or city governments; interest is exempt from federal income tax.

mutual funds: Professionally managed investments offering diversification and liquidity; money of many individuals is pooled together and invested in a group of stocks and/or bonds.

N

need-based awards: Funding from governments, schools, and other groups or organizations available for some students who show financial need.

needs: Those things we must have to survive, such as food, water, shelter, and clothing.

net pay: Gross pay minus all deductions, or the amount you get to actually take home; also called *take-home pay*.

net worth: The difference between what you own and what you owe.

O

outstanding check: A check that has not yet been returned to the bank for payment.

overdraft: Writing a check for more money than you have in your account; also called *bounced checks*.

overdraft protection: The bank pays your check even if you do not have enough in your account to cover it; involves signing up and paying a fee.

overtime wage: The amount paid for working additional hours beyond the standard work week, usually 40 hours.

P

permanent life insurance: A policy that lasts for the life of the individual or as long as premiums are paid.

post-dated check: A check with a date that is in the future.

preferred stock: Stock that has first claim on assets if the company fails; earns dividends but has no voting privileges.

premium: The amount you pay for insurance.

principal: The amount invested or the balance owed on a loan.

private mortgage insurance (PMI): Required by lenders to insure payment if borrower defaults on a mortgage when down payment is less than 20%.

professional development: Improving or gaining new skills related to work.

proprietary school: A privately owned institution that offers various programs and degrees such as business, modeling, paramedical training, and tax preparation.

R

recession: Occurs when stock prices fall and unemployment rises.

rental property: Real estate that is rented or leased to generate income.

renters insurance: Insurance that covers you for theft or damage to the contents of your apartment.

Reserve Officers' Training Corps (ROTC): A military program on many college campuses providing leadership training for commissioned officers; graduates of ROTC become officers in a branch of the military.

retirement account: A savings account specifically set up for later years when you do not want to work full time.

revolving credit: Credit cards that do not require payment in full each month; interest is charged on the unpaid balance.

risk: The possibility that an unfavorable situation could happen to you or to something you own.

rollover: The transfer of retirement funds to a new account.

Roth IRA: An individual retirement account that does not have tax-deferred contributions; but distributions are tax-free under certain conditions.

rule of 72: An equation that estimates how long it will take to double your investment.

S

salary: A set amount of money paid to someone in exchange for work.

savings & loan association: Offers savings accounts, CDs, and checking account services and earns money to pay interest on accounts by issuing home mortgages.

scholarship: College funds based on financial need or some other type of merit or accomplishment which do not have to be repaid; some are based on ACT or SAT scores; others relate to grades, extracurricular activities, athletics, music or other criteria.

secured debt: Debt backed by collateral, such as a car or home.

security: A document that shows evidence of ownership or debt.

security deposit: An amount required for leased property as assurance that the property will be in good condition when you return it.

seminar: A meeting or conference for exchanging ideas or learning new things.

service charge: A fee the bank charges for having an account.

simple interest: Interest that does not compound.

Social Security: A social insurance program run by the U.S. government providing benefits for retired workers, disabled, and other qualified persons.

socially responsible: Being concerned for those around you.

state income taxes: Taxes on income collected by state governments, used to pay for state government, roads, education, and other services.

stock: A share of ownership in a company.

stock market: Where stocks are bought and sold; also called *stock exchange*.

stock split: An increase in the number of shares without changing the total value of the shares; usually a sign of company growth.

supplement: An extra amount above what you have invested and saved for retirement.

T

talent: A natural aptitude or ability to do something that comes easily to you.

tax deductible: An amount that reduces your taxable income.

tax deferred: Retirement accounts on which no taxes are paid on the money put into the account, but tax will be paid when withdrawn.

term life insurance: A policy that provides coverage only for a specific period of time.

time card: A record of the time you start work, the time you leave, and any breaks you take.

trade school: A school that focuses more on skills than academics; sometimes called a vocational school or career and technical college; preparation for careers such as art/design/ fashion, massage therapy, criminal justice, auto technician, nurses' assistant, plumber, electrician, and others.

trust: A legal document that authorizes a trustee to manage your estate on your behalf.

U

U.S. savings bonds: Bonds issued in increments of $25 to $10,000 by the U.S. treasury, backed by the U.S. government.

umbrella policy: Insurance that covers losses above the limits of your other policies; usually for $1 million or more.

unsecured debt: Borrowing money or purchasing goods or services by just signing your name; not backed by a specific asset.

unsecured loan: See *unsecured debt*.

V

values: Your beliefs about ideas and principles that are important to you.

variable expenses: Expenses that change from month to month, such as cell phone bills or personal care items.

W

wage: A dollar amount per hour that you get paid for doing work.

wants: Things we desire but are not necessary to our survival.

wealth: A plentiful supply of money or valuable goods; a wealthy person may be called prosperous or affluent.

will: A legal document that states who will receive your assets when you die.

work-study programs: Part-time jobs on campus often funded by the school or government.

Index

401(k), 251–254
    definition, 251
403(b), 254–255
    definition, 254
529 plan, 171

A

academic degree, 167
account fees, 107
adjustable rate mortgage (ARM), 201–202
    definition, 201
allowances, 41
amortization, 198
annual and lifetime earnings, 167
annual earnings, 167
annual percentage rate (APR), 123
annual percentage yield (APY), 98
apartment, renting, 196
apartment lease, 196
ARM, 201
assessment, 203
assets, 13
ATM, 101
    withdrawals, 103–104
auto calculator, 191
auto insurance, 144–146
    application, 142
    policy, 146
available credit, 127
average rate of return, 18–23
    compound interest, 19–23
    definition, 18

B

bank accounts, 105–106
    ATM withdrawals, 103–104
    certificates of deposit, 97–100
    checking accounts, 83–94
    common, 83–101
    debit cards, 101–104
    money market accounts, 100–101
    savings accounts, 94–97
bank cards. See debit card
banking, 81–113
    common bank accounts, 83–101
    FDIC insurance, 104–105
    other financial organizations, 106–108
bankruptcy, 131–133
    definition, 131
bear market, 212
being Financially Responsible, 25, 54, 108, 124, 159, 180, 195, 221, 255, 273
beneficiary, 154
benefits, 53–54
    bereavement days, 54
    definition, 53
    emergency days, 53
    personal days, 53
    sick days, 53
    vacation pay, 53
benefits statements, 241
bereavement days, 54
blue chip stocks, 213–214
bonds, 223–227
    definition, 223
bounced checks. See overdraft
budgeting, 60–80
    budgets, 62–63
    creating, 72–75
    expenses, 63–67
    income, 68–71
    tips, 74
budgeting software, 74
budgets, 62–63
    definition, 62
bull market, 212

C

calculating earnings, 32–34
calculating net pay, 52
capacity, 116
capital, 118
car insurance, 140–146
    safe-driving course, 140
    types, 141
car lease, 193
car loan application, 188
car ownership, 187–195
    car loan application, 188
    financing, 190–192
    leasing, 193–195
    loans, 187–195
car values, 192
career and technical colleges. See trade school
career choices, 166
cash advances, 127–129
    definition, 127
categorizing expenses, 64
certificates of deposit, 97–100
    definition, 97
chapter 7 bankruptcy, 131
chapter 13 bankruptcy, 131
charitable contributions, 268–273
    definition, 269
    making contributions, 269–270
    volunteering, 271–273
charities, 270
check cards. See debit card
check register, 91–94
    definition, 88
checking accounts, 83–94
    definition, 83
citizenship, 270
COBRA, 148
collateral, 123, 187
college access, 177
college budget, 173–174

college or university education, 167–169
collision coverage, 141
common stock, 210
community college, 169
compound interest, 19–23
    definition, 19
comprehensive coverage, 141
condominium buying, 203
contributions,
    definition, 51, 244
    making, 269–270
corporate bonds, 223
cosigner, 116
costs for school, 174
coupon rate, 223
credit, 114–137
    bankruptcy, 131–133
    capacity, 116
    capital, 118
    character, 116
    credit bureaus, 119–123
    credit cards, 123–130
credit application, 116
credit bureau,
    definition, 119
    credit reports, 119
    FICO credit score, 119
credit card, 123–130
    cash advances, 127–129
    credit card fees, 129–130
    credit card statements, 130–131
    definition, 123
    handling, 124
    purchases, 124–127
    responsibility, 133
credit card application, 117
credit card fees, 129–130
credit card payment calculator, 126
credit card statements, 130–131
credit history, 116
credit report, 119
    application, 120
credit score, 119
credit unions, 106–107
    definition, 106

D

debit cards, 101–104
    definition, 101
    purchases, 101–103
deductible, 141
deductions,
    calculating mandatory, 39–50
    definition, 39
    federal income taxes, 40–43
    local income taxes, 47–48
    Medicare taxes, 44–45
    net pay, 48–49
    Social Security taxes, 43–44
    state income taxes, 45–46
default, 116
deposit slip, 85
deposit slips and checks, 84
depreciation, 187
direct deposit, 49

disability insurance, 153
discretionary income, 71
disposable income. See discretionary income
distribution, 244
diversification, 214
dividend, 201
dollar-cost averaging, 228
Dollars and $ense, 10, 49, 75, 84, 133, 146, 177, 197, 231, 251, 270
    auto insurance policy, 146
    budgeting, 75
    citizenship, 270
    college access, 177
    first investment, 231
    identity theft, 84
    ready for a credit card, 133
    renting your first place, 197
    Roth IRA, 251
    SMART goals, 10
    using direct deposit, 49
donation. See contributions

E

earned income, 245
earnings,
    calculating, 32–34
    wages, 32–33
education, 164–184
    college/university, 167–169
    funding, 171–177
    higher education, 167–171
    lifelong learning, 177–180
    military, 171
    preparing for, 180
    trade schools, 170
    two-year schools, 169
    your career, 166–167
electronic banking, 88
emergency days, 53
entrepreneur, 265–266
    definition, 265
equity, 197
escrow account, 198
estate, 156
estate planning, 156–159
    definition, 156
    trusts, 158–159
    wills, 157–158
ethics, 270
executor, 157
expansion, 212
expenses, 63–67
    definition, 63

F

face value, 154
FDIC insurance, 104–105
Federal Deposit Insurance Corporation (FDIC), 105
federal income taxes, 40–43
    definition, 40
fees, credit cards, 129–130
FICO credit score, 119
FICO scores, 121

filing bankruptcy. See bankruptcy
financial advantages, home buying, 200
financial aid application, 179
financial backing, 265
financial calculator, 25, 126, 191
financial future, 261–276
    average rate of return, 18–23
    building wealth, 13–15
    charitable contributions, 268–273
    financial independence, 267–268
    investing, 16–17
    investment portfolio, 263–266
    planning, 7–29
    Rule of 72, 24–25
financial goals, 9–10, 273
financial independence, 267–268
    definition, 16, 267
    investment pyramid, 267
Financial IQ, 8, 31, 61, 82, 115, 139, 165, 186, 209, 239, 262
financial organizations, 106–108
    credit unions, 106–107
    savings and loan associations, 106
financial plan, 9
financial planning, 9–13
    financial goals, 9–10
    needs and wants, 11
fiscal responsibility, 268
fixed expenses, 63
fixed rate mortgage, 198–200
    definition, 198
fluctuations, 212
foreclosure, 197
form W-4, 41
franchise, 265–266
    definition, 265
franchise fee, 265
fringe benefits. See benefits
FSA accounts, 153
funding, 176
funding of education, 171–177
    potential sources, 172

G

gift, 269
Give It a Go, 12, 15, 34, 42, 52, 64, 67, 70, 72, 84, 91–94, 107, 117, 118, 120, 142, 149, 154, 167, 173–174, 176, 179, 188, 196, 201, 213, 218, 228, 230, 247, 265, 266, 271, 272
    account fees, 107
    auto insurance application, 142
    calculating net pay, 52
    car loan application, 188
    career choices, 166
    categorizing expenses, 64
    check register, 91–94
    college budget, 173–174
    creating a budget, 72
    credit card application, 117
    credit report application, 120

Index

deposit slips and checks, 84
entrepreneurs, 266
federal income taxes, 42–43
financial aid application, 179
funding, 176
insurance plan, 155
inventory, 149
investment portfolio, 228
money smart, 272
mortgage payments, 201
net worth, 15
rental property, 265
renting an apartment, 196
saving for investments, 230
stock market report, 213
three Cs of credit, 118
time card, 34
track stocks, 218
tracking your income, 70
tracking your spending, 67
values, wants, and needs, 12–13
withdrawing money from an IRA, 247
your talents, 271
grace period, 125
grant, 172
gross pay, 32
   calculating, 33
growth, 17, 215–218
   definition, 17, 215

H

HSA accounts, 153
health and disability insurance, 148–153
   disability insurance, 153
   HMO plans, 149
   medical accounts, 152
   POS plans, 150–152
   PPO plans, 149
health insurance, 148
   nonsmokers, 150
health maintenance organization (HMO), 149
health savings accounts, 153
HMO plans, 149
home buying, 197–202
   financial advantages, 200
homeowners association (HOA) fee, 203
homeowners insurance, 146–147
   definition, 146
housing, 195–203
   adjustable rate mortgage, 201–202
   buying a condo, 203
   buying a home, 197–202
   fixed rate mortgage, 198–200
   renting living space, 196–197

I

identity theft, 84
income, 68–71
   average monthly income, 68–70
   definition, 68
   discretionary income, 71
individual retirement account (IRA), 245
Inheritance laws, 158
installment loan, 187
insurance, 50, 138–163
   definition, 140
   estate planning, 156–159
   health and disability insurance, 148–153
   life insurance, 154–155
   looking to buy insurance, 159
   property insurance, 140–148
   types, 156
insurance plan, 154
intestate, 157
investing, 16–17, 210
   definition, 16
   growth, 17
investment, 208–237
   bonds, 223–227
   comparisons, 222
   investing now, 227–231
   mutual funds, 221–222
   saving, 230
investment examples, 17
investment portfolio, 263–266
   definition, 228
   owning your own business, 265–266
   rental property, 263–265
investment pyramid, 267
IRAs, 245–255
   definition, 245
   Roth IRA, 248–251
   withdrawing money, 247

L

leasing a car, 193–195
   buy or lease comparison, 194
lessee, 193
lessor, 193
liabilities, 13
liability coverage, 141
life insurance, 154–155
   definition, 154
   nonsmokers, 155
   permanent insurance, 154–155
   term life, 154
lifelong learning, 177–180
   daily living, 178
   definition, 177
   for career, 177–178
   personal interests, 178
lifetime earnings, 167
liquid, 83
living space, renting, 196–197
living will, 158

loans, 185–207
   car loans, 187–193
   first car, 187–195
local income taxes, 47–48

M

market correction, 212
medical accounts, 152
Medicare, 44
   taxes, 44–45
mentor, 178
military, 171
money market accounts, 100–101
   definition, 100
mortgage, 197
   calculator, 202
   payments, 201
municipal bonds, 224
mutual funds, 221
   definition, 221

N

National College Access Program Directory, 177
National Credit Union Share Insurance Fund (NCUSIF), 106
need-based awards, 174
needs, 11
needs and wants, 11
net pay, 48–49
   definition, 48
net worth, 13, 15

O

online classes, 169
outstanding check, 103
overdraft, 88
overdraft protection, 89
overtime,
   salaries, 37–39
   tips, 36–37
   wages, 39
overtime wage, definition, 34

P

pay yourself first, 72
paychecks, 30–59
   benefits, 53–54
   calculating earnings, 32–34
   mandatory deductions, 39–50
   overtime, 34–39
   verify, 54
   voluntary deductions, 50–52
penalty fees, credit card statements, 130
permanent insurance, life, 154–155
permanent life insurance, definition, 154

personal days, 53
personal identification number (PIN), 103
point of service (POS) plans, 150–152
POS plans, 150–152
post-dated check, 89
PPO plans, 149
preferred provider organization (PPO), 149
preferred stock, 210
premium, 141
principal, 19
private mortgage insurance (PMI), 198
professional development, 177
property insurance, 140–148
    car insurance, 140–146
    homeowners insurance, 146–147
    renters insurance, 148
    umbrella policies, 147
proprietary school, 169
put and take accounts. See checking accounts

R

recession, 212
reconciliation, 90, 94
rental property, 263–265
    definition, 263
renters insurance, 148
repossession of car, 187
research corporations, stocks, 211
Reserve Officers Training Corps (ROTC), 171
retirement account, definition, 50
retirement accounts, 244–255
    401(k), 251–254
    IRAs, 245–255
retirement for teens, 254
retirement planning, 238–260
    retirement accounts, 244–255
    Social Security, 240–244
    teens, 255
revolving credit, 124
risk, 140
rollover, 253
Roth IRA, 248–251
rule of 72, 24–25, 215
    definition, 24

S

salaries, 37–39
salary, 37
savings accounts, 94–97
savings and loan association, 106

scholarship, 172
secured debt, 187
security, 210
security deposit, 193
seminar, 178
service charge, 83
sick days, 53
simple interest, 20
SMART goals, 10
Social Security, 43–44, 240–244
    benefits, 243–244
    definition, 43, 240
    taxes, 43–44
socially responsible, 270
sources of funding education, 172
state income taxes, 45–46
statement of earnings, 241
stock market, 201
stock market report, 212
stock split, 219–221
    definition, 219
stocks, 210–221
    buying, 210–214
    definition, 210
    dividends, 218–219
    reasons to invest, 215–221
    stock splits, 219–221
supplement, 241
surplus. See discretionary income

T

talent, 271
tax deductible, 269
tax deferred, 244
teaser rates, 130
term life insurance, 154
three Cs of credit, 116, 118
thrift and loan. See savings and loan association
time card, 33–34
tips, 36–37
tracking your income, 70
tracking your spending, 67
trade school, 170
trusts, 158–159
    definition, 158
Truth in Lending Disclosure statement, 130

U

U.S. savings bonds, 225
umbrella policy, 147
underwater, 193
unemployment taxes, 49
United States Distance Learning Association (USDLA), 169

unsecured debt, 187
unsecured loan, 123
upside down, 193

V

vacation pay, 53
values, 11
values, wants, and needs, 12–13
variable expenses, 63
vocational schools. See trade school
voluntary deductions, calculating, 50–52
    contributions, 51
    insurance, 50
    savings or retirement accounts, 50
volunteering, 271–273

W

wage, definition, 32
wages, 32–33, 39, 169
wants, 11
wants and needs, 11
wealth, 13
wealth, building, 13–15
Web Connect, 23, 25, 39, 46–47, 74, 105–106, 121, 126, 130, 144–145, 153, 158, 169, 174, 192, 202, 211, 243–244, 250, 254, 266, 270
    auto insurance, 144–145
    bank accounts, 105–106
    budgeting software, 74
    car values, 192
    charities, 270
    costs for school, 174
    current interest rates, 23
    FICO scores, 121
    financial calculator, 126
    financial calculators, 25
    franchises, 266
    health savings accounts, 153
    inheritance laws, 158
    mortgage calculator, 202
    research corporations, 211
    retirement for teens, 254
    Roth IRAs, 250
    Social Security benefits, 243–244
    state income tax rates, 46–47
    Truth in Lending, 130
    wages, 39, 169
weekly spending record, 65
will, 157
workers' compensation, 153
work-study programs, 174